America
ENTERTAINS
a year of imaginative parties

America

ENTERTAINS

a year of imaginative parties

DAVID TUTERA

photographs by Ericka McConnell

stewart, tabori & chang • new york

Published in 2003 by
Stewart, Tabori & Chang
A Company of La Martinière Groupe
115 West 18th Street
New York, NY 10011

Export Sales to all countries except Canada, France,
and French-speaking Switzerland:
Thames and Hudson Ltd.
181A High Holborn
London WC1V 7QX
England

Library of Congress Cataloging-in-Publication Data
Tutera, David
   America entertains : a year of imaginative parties / author, David Tutera.
   ISBN 1-58479-284-1
   1. Parties. I. Title

TX731.T86 2003
793.2–dc21   2003045840

Design by Nina Barnett

The text of this book was composed in New Baskerville and Rotis Sans Serif

Printed in Singapore

10 9 8 7 6 5 4 3 2 1

First Printing

Acknowledgments

When I think of my experience creating *America Entertains*, the words that come to mind are passion, excitement, creativity, simplicity, and challenge. While producing this book, I was privileged to enjoy a wonderful journey across a magnificent country. I am a blessed individual because my work is all about bringing happiness and joy into peoples' lives—tears of joy at weddings, gleaming smiles of happiness at anniversary parties—and the chance to create a lifetime of memories at each of the special occasions I am fortunate to touch.

None of this would be possible without the unconditional love and nurturing of my mom and dad, Jo Ann and Joe Tutera. My parents each provided me with guidance, love, and creativity as a child and allowed me to explore the arts so I could tap into every facet of my own creativity. Without this freedom and without their love, I wouldn't have been able to turn my clients' fantasies into reality. Without my parents' support, I would not have been able to write this book, or share my entertaining ideas with such enthusiasm. I thank each member of my family—Gregg, Amy, Rich, Mia, Pop-Pop, Nanny, Maria, Vergie, and Scott—for your continued support.

From the bottom of my heart, I would like to thank my partner in life, my soul mate and angel, Ryan Jurica. Each step of our lives we take together, and it is you that enables me to grow and challenge myself. Thank you, Ryan, for all of your brilliant and original ideas, as well as your unconditional love. You are always there for me. I would not have been able to create this book without you, your recipes, and all of your talents.

My entire staff poured a great deal of their artistry and time into this book as well. I thank each of you—Shawn Rabideau, Diane Wagner, Sal Pontillo, Debbie Rossi, Steve Skopick, and Lisa Bass—for your help executing my ideas.

I want to thank Fredi Freidman, my literary agent, for your hard work and for standing beside me and my vision. Your insight, direction, and sincere care mean so much to me.

To Ceridwen Morris: Your patience, creativity, and brilliant words have made this project not only a joy but a breeze to complete. You have made this entire book such fun and a collection of stories never to be forgotten. You are a gem and I look forward to working with you on the next book, which is right around the corner.

Ericka McConnell's photography has captured all of my ideas and made them look stunning on paper. Thank you, Ericka, for your patience and for providing your talents to this book.

Thank you to each and every one of you at Stewart, Tabori & Chang for working so hard on this project, for making it look so wonderful, and for respecting my opinions and vision. I truly appreciate each of you: Leslie Stoker, Sarah Scheffel, Nina Barnett, Jack Lamplough, and Leda Scheintaub.

A special thank you to each of the restaurants and chefs that provided the unique and wonderful collection of recipes in this book.

I would also like to express my gratitude to the following friends: Barbara and Steven Davis of Cloth Connection, Carol and Joey Low, Nat Nugget and The Pleasantdale Chateau, Banfi Vineyards, Arlyn and Ed Gardner, Susan Laufer, Diane and Mark Lehman, Pat Dammerman and Heather Wesoloski, Terri Bartlett, Sandy Cattani, The Giraffe Hotel, Tomar Studios, Ruth Fishel Linens, Westside Party Rentals, Marc Blackwell, Gallery 849, Abigail's, Props for Today, Unique Table Tops, Sweet Lisa's Cakes, and Laura Leigh of Alpine Creative Group.

Thank you also to models Jonathan Agami, Michael Alge, Lars Anderson, Adam Bassano, Eric Breitbard, Cynthia and Franck Bismuth, Dwayne Britton, Caroline A. Enright, Tom Fitzpatrick, Ronalyn Garcia, Eden Gattullo, Richard Gigler, Kate Gigler, Amy Grall, Mia Grall, Richard Grall, Catherine L. Jhung, Peter Jones, Jennifer Joy, Anthony LaMont, Lisa Lippman, Alexis Mentor, Alexandra Mikaelian, Laurie Miller-Donnis, Jennifer Noble, Amit Patel, Lucas di Porzio, Mollie Ragusa, Trevor Richardson, Alex Rodriquez, Julia Santoro, Stephanie Santoro, Elaine Schiebel, Galen Smith, Carole Sylvan, Anna Vinokourooa, Lara Voss, Beverly Warren, and Genevieve Welch.

Happy Entertaining!

Contents

Introduction

As a party planner, I transport party guests to another world. I've been called an artist, a magician, a Broadway impresario—even a therapist. I'm the middleman between a client's fascination with horses and the perfect saddle leather placemats that set the table at her dinner party. My job is to take a vague notion of whimsy and make it come to life with a room full of marabou feather boas. Anything's possible. I've turned the John F. Kennedy Center for the Performing Arts into a whimsical garden with lavender lights and ivy "growing" up the chandeliers. When clients such as Elton John, Barbara Walters, the Prince of Wales, and the Rolling Stones ask me to design their events, I know they want something spectacular. They want me to create a world that their guests will long remember.

My reputation is built on the grand, elaborate parties I've staged. But my eighteen years in the business have also taught me one constant about all parties: Home is where the heart is, and great parties are all about heart. All too often people think that the keys to a successful party are a fancy hotel ballroom, an expensive catering team, and engraved invitations. These details do have a place in the world of extravagant entertaining, but all the baked Brie and custom-made linens on Earth cannot substitute for the kind of character that can only come to parties from people and the places where they live. And as I can attest after traveling around the country producing everything from gala affairs to intimate dinners for two, America is literally bursting at the seams with just this kind of character. Whether it's a bartender reinventing the world's very first cocktail, the Sazerac, in New Orleans or a native Charlestonian passing down her Aunt Bunny's recipe for a Sloe Gin Fizz, these are small treasures of our collective culture. Likewise, the Chicago lawyer who spikes her Thanksgiving mashed potatoes with wasabi unwittingly starts a new family tradition, and the Miami artist who replaces wine and crudités with fried plantains and mint-infused martinis redefines the standard art-opening fare. It is, after all, the small expressions of individual tastes and regions that together make up a nation of traditions as diverse and original as America's.

My first book, *A Passion for Parties,* was written to serve as an essential primer for anyone interested in hosting great parties, from Bar Mitzvahs to baby showers. This book certainly touches upon many of these kinds of special occasions, but it also explores and celebrates the diverse flavors, personalities, and cultures found in our own backyard. From the severe seascapes of Nantucket to Miami's lush, tropical gardens, the American landscape displays all the verve and variety you'd expect from an entire continent. And from New Age Santa Fe to the sensual Southern style of historic Charleston, American traditions, cuisines, and lifestyles perfectly express their specific environments as well as a universal idea of what it is to be an American. I have tried to distill the knowledge and experience I've gained from hosting events across the nation into sixteen parties inspired by twelve different states, taking readers on an unforgettable road trip that stretches from a Washington, D.C., garden party to a romantic ranch wedding party under the big Texas sky, while hitting all the high points in between.

Each party in this book is organized into what I call the "Three E's": the "Essentials," the "Extras," and the "Extravagances." The "Essentials" are the easily achieved techniques for creating the right atmosphere. Maybe it's something as simple as featuring a specific kind of flower, a color scheme, or a choice of wine. For Miami it might be the sounds of Cuban samba; for Santa Fe, a few glazed ceramic bowls filled with mountain flowers and aloe vera. The "Extras" are for splurging a little, making the chocolate-dipped rose petals for Valentine's Day in New Orleans, or serving a chic, imported sake for an East-meets-West Thanksgiving. For a once-in-a-lifetime (or decade) blowout, there are the "Extravagances:" The crimson seventeenth-century velvet tablecloth; the custom-designed Lucite runner filled with tropical flowers; the massive hanging lampshades covered with feathers; the carpets of rose petals. I always provide a range of possibilities for my client: the best, the better, and the best of the better. Using the "Three E's" is a fast way to determine which level meets both the budget and the time constraint.

Each chapter also features ten "Tutera Tips." Tutera Tips are practical, though often innovative, ideas that can be applied to a specific event, then used over and over again for many different events. My tips range from the sensible ("how to clean your grill") to the magical ("how to make suspended floral pom-poms for a black-and-white ball"). Essentially, they are valuable tidbits that I've developed afters years of trial-and-error. At this stage in the game, if I don't have a good solution for how to deal with the New Year's Eve coat pile-up, or where to seat your most eccentric relatives at a reception, I might as well call it a day. The tips cover all aspects of entertaining, from invitations to décor and atmosphere, from entertainment to cocktails and food.

Speaking of food, a few words on the recipes and menus in this book. I grew up in a household where both of my parents loved to cook, especially on the holidays. Whether I was acting as sous chef for my dad on Thanksgiving, weeping over a chopping board of yellow onions, or helping Mom crush bag after bag of fresh walnuts for her famous chocolate chip cookies, I was always happy to be in the kitchen during the days or hours preceding a big party. Laughter, as well as the unmistakable aromas of lovingly prepared food, filled the house every time my parents entertained.

I still believe that there's nothing quite like a terrific meal at home shared with family and friends. That said, I am not a professional chef, and as much as I'd love to reel off my favorite personal recipes, I'm always compelled to pick up new culinary tricks from the masters. I may know a thing or two about table settings, food and drink presentation, the timing of meals, and the progression of courses, but I always turn to the experts when it comes to the recipes and food preparation. Just as I seek out excellent caterers for the events I produce, I have combed this country for twelve knockout chefs to help me concoct the fantastic regional recipes you will find in this book.

From the famous Hotel Jerome in Aspen (where Todd Slossberg delivers Ruby Red Trout Hash and more for breakfast) to Emeril's Restaurant (where Christopher Wilson crafted the recipes for the mouthwatering, sensual feast for my Gothic Saint Valentine's Day party), my tour of some of the best restaurants in this country has resulted in twelve inspired menus. I worked with each chef to create a variety of recipes that combine the essence of local cuisines with contemporary twists and innovative ideas for presentation. In general, I stuck to regional culinary motifs; however, I did make some wild leaps and transformations here and there. In Santa Fe, I opted to work with Mark Kiffin, a fantastic French chef who infuses his cuisine with subtle hints of Southwestern flavors. In Kansas, I corralled my

friends Mike and Debbie, co-owners of 40 Sardines, to rustle up what must be the chicest backyard barbecue ever assembled.

For each party, the chef and I sat down and asked (and answered) all the key catering questions pertinent to the party: What produce is in season? What are the unique regional flavors and foods? How formal is the party and how will the food be served? Can the recipes be made in advance or do they need to be served straight from the stove? We also considered the personality of the hosts, the nature of the celebrations, and the desired atmosphere of the party. The results are astonishing—whether you follow each menu recipe for recipe, or simply try out one dish at a time.

Although these chefs are accustomed to a restaurant staff and kitchen, I can assure you that these recipes can all be easily prepared in your kitchen with ingredients available in local supermarkets. After all, the chefs I worked with may have come up with the recipes, but they did not do the cooking for each of my hosts. So, don't be intimidated. Chances are, a lot of these recipes will become trusted entertaining favorites for you, as they have become for me.

Throughout the writing of this book, I've tried to bottle up the essence of each place I visited in the moment I visited it. However, this is not to say that my ideas for a January dance party in Miami cannot be translated for use at a Philadelphia barbecue in August. In fact, I've tried to describe and represent each party so that you can take a tip from my Thanksgiving in Chicago, a floral design from Memorial Day in Kansas, and maybe a recipe from my New Year's party in Manhattan to create your own original party. There's no end to the possibilities: My "database" of party tips is at your disposal. I hope you have as much fun incorporating my ideas into your own personal style as I've had learning from my clients and contributors. Get out your Post-it notes and don't forget to let your own style guide you. That is, after all, the most thoughtful gesture a host can make; it is the same gesture I've tried to make in the pages of this book.

January in Miami

winter goes south for dinner and drinks

January is all about new beginnings. The cupboards are almost empty of leftover holiday cookies, the last streamer from New Year's Eve has been swept from the floor, and your resolutions are still firm (even if nothing else is!). We all love the baroque trappings of the holiday season, but let's face it, by January 1 we're ready to turn over a new leaf. And at the refreshing, vibrant party I threw in Miami at the beginning of the month, that leaf just happened to be a giant monstera leaf straight from the tropics. These deep green fronds served as bouquets, as placemats, and as fans. They framed glass bowls of chilled mango soup and platters of spicy tapas. And they beckoned guests to indulge in the delights of the smooth Cuban martinis at the bar.

There's no better place to go for this kind of tropical detox than Miami. More than any other city in America, it exemplifies the fresh, the exotic, and the electrifying. It's so far south it's not even really the South anymore. You're more likely to find a Cuban tamale stand than a Waffle House; more likely to tango with a stranger than to fox trot with a debutante. It's the fountain of youth for the young and old alike. But we're not here in search of youth, just its temporary equivalent: Miami is a great place to throw a party.

THE RHYTHM OF THE CITY comes pulsing out of passing convertibles, and if you're in the mood to dance, there's always a beat lingering in the background for an impromptu mambo. The clear white stretches of beach and the grand row of Art Deco hotels are a monument to the simple yet decadent charms of life at the edge of the Earth. And what bartender wouldn't love a place abundant with mangos and coconuts? The drinks practically make themselves! So with all this in mind, I take back what I said before. Miami is not a great place to party; Miami is a party.

Of course there's something even better about Miami: Its chief delights are easily portable. Those amazing crates of navel oranges that your favorite aunt sends you every winter don't come from the North

Pole, they come from Florida. So if you can't convince your travel agent to offer you just a few days of Miami-style R&R, have Miami come to you. With a little help from the farmer's market and FedEx, you can bring the tastes, sounds, and smells of Miami right into your own home, even in the depths of an Ozarks winter. And trust me, when those smooth Cuban standards come through the stereo speakers, the first succulent taste of mango melts in your mouth, and the scent of fresh coconut milk fills the air in your kitchen, you won't be thinking about the snow outside. Add a few gerbera daisies, which are available year-round at a farmer's market or a good florist, and you'll enjoy just a splash of warm color from the islands. Add a few palms or other large, flat leaves to the mix, and you'll start to wonder if the thermostat in your house is set too high.

Of course, the source of heat at the party I threw for Lena and Angelo definitely had something to do with the hosts. In celebration of Lena's (very successful) first solo exhibition of paintings, ten of her friends got together for cocktails and dinner before a night of dancing in South Beach. This scorching couple has lived together in Miami for twenty-five years, and you can see it in everything about them, from the way they move to the clothes they wear to the colorful paintings with which they surround themselves. As Lena passed cocktails to the guests, she was already moving to the music in the background like it was a soundtrack emanating from her very bones. I have always believed that it is essential for the host of a party to be there not only as a guest, but as an inspiration for how to live in that particular moment. And that night, it was definitely Lena's moment.

In the days leading up to the party, Lena and I didn't talk much about what she envisioned. She just told me she wanted the party to be as colorful and energetic as her paintings, yet as cool and simple as her lifestyle with Angelo. I've been to Miami countless times, and every time I go I find a new spark of inspiration, whether I'm admiring the lighting in the lobby of the Delano Hotel or stopping for a Cubano at a beachside cafe. But the prospect of capturing Lena and Angelo in the spirit of a party was a whole new kind of inspiration: They were Miami times ten. It would be modern, it would be sensual, it would be spare, it would be exotic. Deep green palm leaves would fan against white walls; coconuts would be split in half and used as bowls for chilled mango soup; citrus oils, trickling water, and candles floating among bright flowers would ravish the senses; and the sounds of Cuban guitar music would move through the guests like a wave. There would be no tinsel or hot cider at this winter wonderland, but with the Buena Vista Social Club and the Afro-Cuban All Stars playing the score, things would definitely be hot.

A Taste of Cuba

A high-spirited Cuban menu was certainly in store for Lena's red-hot dinner party; the question was where to find the perfect chef in this city full of thriving Cuban restaurants? I can't put my finger on the one reason I selected chef Pedro Maradiago, but I'll never forget the first time I tasted his food. I was sitting on a bongo-shaped stool, grooving to the rhythms of Latin dance music at Gloria and Emilio Estefan's Larios on the Beach, when a plate of Frijoles Rojos was placed before me. The scents rising off this red bean dish were intoxicating, the first bite an explosion of flavors. I could taste a little bit of Cuba (beans), a touch of Africa (cumin), and a dash of Spain (spicy sausage). I knew I'd hit the Miami jackpot. The sauce was complex but ever so subtle, with a perfect balance of sweet and spicy. I learned that this was one of Pedro's signature dishes, and the rest is history.

Pedro created a fantastic menu for Lena's predancing party: those Frijoles Rojos, a traditional Ropa Vieja, and his Sublime Coconut Flan, a real tribute to the tropical. For tapas, we passed fresh mango chutney on crispy, fried plantains. Then, for the first course, two chilled fruit soups would give Lena's guests a cool, refreshing start to a zesty meal. I ladled the soups—tropical mango and wild berry—into halved coconuts one hour before the party began. Lena simply pulled the coconut bowls from the fridge once her guests were seated. The main course was served family style in large, colorful ceramic dishes arranged right on the table. The flan was passed around after dinner on small glass plates, along with little shots of rum and top-ups of champagne to get the crowd ready for some serious dancing—and it worked. Come time to leave for the club, Lena's guests were energized by the spices, and seduced by the berries and coconuts.

Tropical Centerpieces

As far as I know there are no laws on the books for party design, but it should be a crime to decorate a Miami-style party without a nod to the ocean. Can you imagine Miami without its deeply alluring presence? That's what I thought. So even in my earliest plans for the party, I knew the all-important centerpiece had to be wet, and maybe even a little wild. It had to evoke the ocean at night, with its seductive combination of passion, serenity, and mystery. Lucky for me, once the idea was in place, it was surprisingly easy to set the table with a miniature late-night lagoon. I positioned a long, rectangular, watertight Lucite box (about 5 inches deep and 5 feet long) in the center of the table and filled it with water to the depth of a few inches. An abundance of hot pink gerbera daisies, orange pincushions, and a few purple cattleya orchids and the occasional votive candle floated in the shallow pool. The combination of flickering candlelight reflecting off the still water and the bright colored flowers became the visual equivalent of luxuriating in the clear, coral-filled waters off the Florida Keys at midnight, with nothing to light your way but a few burning torches on the beach. I had this particular Lucite box custom designed for Lena's dining table—it was my one extravagance for this party—but you can just set a series of square glass bowls side by side down the center of your table and work your own magic. It might cost half the price, but it will still look like a truly tropical, half-lit oasis.

And speaking of Oasis (a foam used by florists that readily absorbs water), I used some to create gerbera daisy "pom-pom" candleholders for each end of the Lucite runner. They add a lovely height to its general-

ly long, low lines. To make these cheerful floral flourishes, simply submerge a ball of Oasis (about the size of a coconut) into water until it is completely saturated. Slice the bottom quarter of the orb off, creating a flat area on the bottom, and place the ball on a small glass dish. Attach gerbera daisies (with stems cut to 2 inches) by poking them into the soft dome until it is almost completely covered, with only a small space on top left for a candle. Then just insert the candle (I used a mango-scented orange-hued candle), make sure it's stable, and wait for everyone to ask you how you created this breathtaking display.

You can easily buy gerbera daisies year-round, so they serve as an ideal flower for winter entertaining. They are a little fragile, but if you keep them warm and watered, they will positively flourish. I decided to use them for one final gesture at Lena's party, an exotic arrangement in the foyer that set the tone as the guests arrived. You can easily do the same. Put one large bunch of gerbera daisies into a tall glass vase, and watch as the arrangement makes itself. The captivating design of the curving, tube-like stems will prepare your guests for the call of the wild—though things won't really get wild until the dancing starts.

A Few Tropical Flower Arrangements

Any flamboyant, tropical flower will heat up a room on a chilly January night, but these are a few of my favorite blood-warming flower arrangements:

- Fill a vase with just one kind of tropical leaf, such as monstera leaves, areca palms, or bird-of-paradise leaves.

- Bird-of-paradise flowers are tall, slinky stunners. Just add three to a tall glass vase, and try to stop your guests from rubbernecking as they pass them.

- Bougainvillea on the vine, and by itself, is very sexy as it cascades over the sides of its container.

- Hibiscus flowers look wonderful floating in a glass bowl of water.

- Orchids planted in soil, floating in water, or assembled in a vase are always beautiful. And there are so many colors and styles to pick from.

- White and pink anthurium are bold and unique. And they look especially great with a few red or pink ginger flowers around them. In fact, ginger flowers look great mixed with any of the above.

Monstera Leaf Place Settings

A monstera leaf place mat brings the essence of this party directly to each guest's dinner setting. And what a statement it makes: clean, modern, natural, and exotic. And why disrupt such a simple, striking touch with the addition of loud, colorful plates? Nature can speak more dramatically for itself, in this case. And so, to foreground its presence, I used glass plates, square glass "bowls" to hold the halved-coconuts filled with soup, and small glass dishes for the ice-molded shot glasses. The flatware was Lucite, to match the runner. But just one subtle dash of color really finishes off the setting. I folded papaya-colored napkins into squares (echoing the square glass bowls) and tied loose strands of lily grass around the width of them. On the top of each folded napkin I placed one delicate, stemless orchid. This layering of natural elements creates a lush, but unfussy, look.

Of course, place mats aren't the only use for monstera leaves. At Lena and Angelo's, I placed them in a few different spots in the room, creating a series of arrangements that pulled the entire party space together. But just a few of these leaves at the bar and one or two surrounding a plate of tapas make a sleek, unifying statement of their own.

The Art of the Amuse-Bouche

France may be thousands and thousands of miles away from Miami in both distance and spirit, but the French have been perfecting the art of tasting for centuries; they can always teach us a thing or two about eating. Take the amuse-bouche, for instance. This French term literally means "mouth amusement," and refers to a tantalizing, tiny portion of food offered to diners just after they are seated. In fine restaurants all over the world, the amuse-bouche is often served as a small, luxurious gift to excite the senses of favored customers. At your party, all of the guests should feel special, and offering a tiny taste of something interesting soon after they sit down is not only a great way to establish the flavors of the meal, but a wonderful way to make your guests feel absolutely divine.

Unlike an array of appetizers, an amuse-bouche is best when it's pristine and focused, and served with a complementary aperitif. The ambiance and flavor at our party in Miami owed more to Cuba than to Paris, so I served an oversized, golden plantain chip topped with a mound of mango chutney. The sweet fire of the chutney is just right to bring out the faint, lingering sweetness of the plantain, while playing perfectly against its saltiness. Likewise, the smooth, soft texture of the chutney accents the crisp chip—we call matches like this culinary fusion. The coup de grace of this perfectly balanced taste is an aperitif of chilled vodka served in nothing less than a shot glass made of ice. There should be a picture of this pairing right next to the words amuse-bouche in the French dictionary! Its flavors are pure, direct, and enticing. When made with just the right balance of innovation and simplicity amuse-bouches make a lovely, focused statement about the food to come, and promise a sensual meal that will impress with big flavor, not big volume. After all, who wants to go salsa dancing when they feel like they have a Christmas turkey in their stomach? That was last month!

Mango Chutney
with Plantain Chips
(Serves 6 or more)

FOR THE MANGO CHUTNEY
2 large ripe mangoes, peeled, pitted,
   and chopped into ½-inch cubes
1 red onion, peeled and chopped
   into ¼-inch cubes
1 cucumber, peeled, seeded,
   and chopped into ¼-inch cubes
½ bunch cilantro, leaves only, coarsely chopped
1 serrano chile, seeded and minced
Juice of 2 limes (3 to 4 tablespoons)
Salt and freshly ground pepper to taste

FOR THE PLANTAIN CHIPS
2 large plantains
Vegetable oil, for frying
Salt to taste

1. To make the chutney, put the mangoes, onion, cucumber, cilantro, chile, and lime juice in a nonreactive bowl and toss to combine. Cover and refrigerate for at least 1 hour.
2. When it's time to serve, add salt and pepper and toss once more.
3. To make the chips, cut the unpeeled plantains on the diagonal into ⅛-inch-thick slices. After slicing, remove and discard the peels.
4. Heat the oil in a large, heavy-bottom skillet, and when it's hot (350° F), fry the plantain slices until they're golden brown, about 1 minute on each side.
5. Transfer the fried plantains slices to a plate lined with paper towels to drain and add plenty of salt while they're still hot.
6. Let cool, then serve with the chutney on the side.

Milking Coconuts:
ten great things to do with coconut milk

When I think of coconuts, I have to admit that images of Mary Ann and the Skipper using those funny-looking halved and hairy orbs as telephone receivers on Gilligan's Island do come to mind. But this is not to say that coconuts cannot be taken seriously or, for that matter, taken off the desert isle and transported to your living room. In fact, some of my favorite uses for coconut milk are for cold-weather comfort foods such as pies, spicy Thai chili, and in syrup for biscuits. So, in addition to using coconuts for your piña coladas (and as pretend telephones) here are some year-round uses for these white-fleshed treats:

- Substitute coconut milk for cream or milk in coffee or in an ice cream recipe.
- Pour over fresh bananas, strawberries, and granola cereal.
- Use in milk shakes, smoothies, and malts.
- Instead of hot chocolate, warm up a little coconut milk with regular milk.
- Use it to poach fish (especially a light, white fish).
- Freeze it until ice-cold, whip, and serve over pineapple or other fruit-based desserts.
- For very moist and flaky biscuits, substitute coconut milk for water or milk in your favorite biscuit recipe.
- Beat at room temperature until thick lumps appear. Knead lumps together, pouring off whey for excellent butter. Great on biscuits or pancakes.
- Stir a little into cooked rice with some garlic, a couple of chopped chiles, and a few fresh basil leaves for an instant Thai-influenced side dish.
- Add some fresh milk to a hot bath for a tropical, skin-soothing treat.

Making Coconut Milk

This is a wonderful way to work out some tension in the kitchen. I love the fact that the process of culling sweet milk involves a hammer and the sharpest knife in your drawer! It sounds a bit hideous and messy, but it's really quite fun. And worth it: Real coconut milk is heaps better than its canned counterpart. When I was a child my dad used to crack open coconuts and serve us kids chunks of coconut meat. It's this childhood memory that is responsible for my adult affection for these funny fruits!

1. Open the coconut by cracking it open with a hammer.
2. Remove the flesh with a sharp knife.
3. Finely grate the coconut meat.
4. Pour boiling water over the grated coconut to cover.
5. Mix in a food processor or blender. Let sit for 20 to 30 minutes.
6. Strain through cheesecloth and squeeze out as much milk as you can. One coconut yields about $\frac{1}{3}$ cup milk.

Warm Winter Coconut Roast

This is a great snack to serve for movie night or poker night, or in small bowls at a cocktail party. It's an easy, sweet, and surprising alternative to regular warm nuts. It's also a fabulous topping for your favorite dessert. All you need are two coconuts for every four servings.

1. Preheat oven to 325° F.
2. Use an ice pick or another sharp, pointed tool to make at least two holes in each coconut. Drain the coconut milk and reserve it for another use.
3. Put the whole coconut shell in the oven and bake it for 1 hour.
4. Let the shell cool for 30 minutes to 1 hour, then tap it with a hammer until it cracks. Use a knife to break off the chunks of warm coconut meat. Cut the softened coconut meat into thin slices—the thinner the better—and spread them on a baking sheet.
5. Bake at 200° F for 2 hours, frequently tossing the coconut flakes with tongs.
6. Remove from the oven and serve immediately as a snack or as the topping to your favorite dessert.

Hot Shots

Tropical drinks involve lots of ice whether crushed or in cubes, but how about serving your aperitifs in shot glasses made from ice? The mold, available at party supply stores, is called "Shot Rocks." On a scorching hot day they may become a little slippery to handle, but on a regular Miami January night (or on a January night anywhere north of Miami) these little ice cups are a great way to kick off cocktail hour. In keeping with the cool, liquid motif of this party I served chilled Belvedere vodka and garnished each glass with a little shaved coconut and a tropical flower.

Cuban Martini

1 teaspoon sugar
3 sprigs fresh mint, plus additional leaves
* for garnish*
1 ounce fresh lime juice (about 1 lime)
2 ounces vodka (my brand is Belvedere)
A splash of Moët & Chandon Champagne

1. Use a muddler to grind the sugar, mint, and lime juice together in the bottom of a cocktail shaker.
2. Add ice cubes and the vodka, then shake and strain into a well-chilled martini glass.
3. Top with the splash of Champagne.
4. Garnish with a mint leaf.

Three E's

Essentials
- Monstera Leaves
- Cuban Martinis
- Cuban Samba

Extras
- Cattleya Orchids
- Amuse-Bouches or Tapas
- Palm Trees

Extravagances
- Custom Lucite Runner
- Carved-Ice Shot Glasses
- Cuban Cigars

TUTERA TIPS

• Transform a clear glass vase into a swirling, patterned one by wrapping tropical leaves (such as ti leaves) around the interior of the vase. These leaves are so big that they will cling to the inside walls of the glass instead of floating and drifting away.

• Use citrus fruit as a refreshing decorative element: Fill glass bowls, in a variety of sizes, with limes, lemons, and oranges. What a great, inexpensive way to fill a room with color!

• Substitute gerbera daisies with orchids, roses, or gardenias in your floating centerpiece. Avoid lilies, as they are top-heavy and do not balance well in water.

• Clean wax-covered glass votives by freezing them for a day. The extreme cold helps loosen the wax so that you can pop the candle remains out and reuse the votives.

• Make a tea-candle holder from a halved and scooped-out lemon. Slice a large fresh lemon in half, and slice off the tip of the lemon rind, creating a flat base for the lemon to stand on. Using a paring knife and a spoon, remove the pulp and insert a tea light.

• Use hollowed-out oranges, lemons, and limes as sorbet bowls. Take the half shell of the citrus fruit and fill with sorbet of the same or complementary flavor. Then refreeze and serve when ready.

• To create an inexpensive and simple invitation for a tropical party, start by printing your information on a simple yellow panel card. Then glue the yellow card onto a slightly larger hot pink card and then glue the pink card onto a slightly larger orange card.

• When hosting a party intended to continue on to clubs for dancing (or to another event) hire a car service for the evening. This will ease transitions, save time, and prevent guests from feeling like they're chauffeuring themselves. Remember to always drink responsibly!

• Use coffee filters or newspaper to clean a glass table. The filters or newspaper will leave a lint-free and streak-free shine.

• Create square chunks of lime (like lime "cubes") for cocktail garnishes. Remove the peel from a lime and cut the fruit into small, precise squares. Add to water or cocktails for a wonderful geometric look.

¡Hasta Luego Miami!

I don't know if any of the guests noticed that the bright pink gerbera daisies in the centerpiece matched the original Warhol silk screens hanging on the wall, let alone that the Lucite runner perfectly complemented their Plexiglas frames. But I know that when the sun went down, all eyes were on the floating flowers illuminated by flickering votives. I got firsthand news from Lena that a whole new series of paintings was inspired by the warm peach glow wavering across the faces of her friends, the flowers, and the food. It wasn't the fact that my party lighting concepts would be immortalized in a great work of art (though it's nothing to sneeze at) that pleased me most about hearing this news. It was the knowledge that the most inspiring things about the party were things that anyone could enjoy anywhere. And even if the only thing you take from this party is the vision of a few striking palms, a dramatic arrangement of hot pink flowers, and a dollop of mango salsa on a crisp fried plantain, you're half way to Miami. And you've certainly warmed up your neck of the woods.

January in Miami
MENU

Courtesy of Pedro Maradiago,
chef at Larios on the Beach.

Chilled Tropical Mango Soup

Cold Wild Berry Soup

Frijoles Rojos

Ropa Vieja

Sublime Coconut Flan

Chilled Tropical Mango Soup
(Serves 6)

4 very ripe mangoes (about 2½ pounds)
1 cup fresh orange juice
¾ cup sugar
4 whole cloves
1 tablespoon small-grain tapioca
1 cup unsweetened coconut milk
¼ cup Malibu Rum (it's coconut-flavored)
1 cup dry white wine, chilled
2 tablespoons honey

TO SERVE
3 coconuts (optional)
Shredded coconut
Lime slices

Peel, pit, and coarsely chop the mangoes. Place them in a food processor and puree until smooth, then set aside.

In a saucepan, combine 1 cup water, the orange juice, sugar, cloves, and tapioca. Stirring occasionally, bring the mixture to a boil over medium heat. Reduce the heat to low and simmer, stirring constantly, until the mixture becomes thick, about 15 minutes. Add the pureed mango and the coconut milk, rum, wine, and honey; stir until well combined, about 2 minutes.

Remove from the heat and carefully strain the mixture through a fine-mesh sieve or chinois into a bowl, then set the bowl in a larger bowl filled with ice water. When the soup is cool, remove it from the ice-water bath, cover, and refrigerate for at least 1 hour.

If you're serving the soup in coconut shells, cut the coconuts in half through the equator—a cleaver works best—and discard the coconut water or save for another use. Ladle each serving of soup into half a coconut shell, then top with shredded coconut and garnish with a lime slice.

Cold Wild Berry Soup

(Serves 6)

1 cup raspberries, fresh, or frozen, thawed
1 cup blueberries, fresh, or frozen, thawed
2 cups strawberries, fresh, or frozen, thawed,
  hulled, and halved
½ cup cranberry-strawberry juice cocktail
½ cup dry white wine
¼ cup sugar
Juice of ½ lime (about 1½ tablespoons juice)
⅛ teaspoon cinnamon
⅛ teaspoon allspice
One 8-ounce container strawberry yogurt,
  or ½ cup heavy cream

TO SERVE
3 coconuts (optional)
Fresh berries, if available
Lime slices

Place the raspberries, blueberries, strawberries, and juice cocktail in a blender and blend on medium speed until smooth. Strain the berry mixture through a fine-mesh sieve or chinois into a saucepan. Add the wine, sugar, lime juice, cinnamon, and allspice and bring to a boil over medium heat; stirring continuously, boil for 1 minute.

Remove the soup from the heat and transfer it to a bowl set in a larger bowl filled with ice water. When the soup is cool, remove it from the ice-water bath, cover, and refrigerate for at least 1 hour.

Just before serving the soup, stir in the yogurt. If you're serving the soup in coconut shells, cut the coconuts in half through the equator—a cleaver works best—and discard the coconut water or save for another use. Ladle each serving of soup into half a coconut shell, then top with a fresh berry or two, if available, and garnish with a lime slice.

Frijoles Rojos

(Serves 6 or more)

1 pound dried red beans
¼ pound slab bacon, cut into chunks
½ pound ham, cut into ½-inch cubes
2 Spanish chorizo sausages, cut into ½-inch pieces
  (about ½ pound)
1 pound potatoes, peeled and cut into 1-inch cubes
1 pound zucchini, chopped
¼ head cabbage, coarsely chopped
1 red onion, chopped
1 green bell pepper, seeded and sliced
1 tablespoon salt
1 tablespoon freshly ground pepper
1 teaspoon ground cumin
One 8-ounce can tomato sauce
3 coconuts (optional)

Rinse the beans and put them in a bowl with enough water to cover the beans by several inches. Soak for 3 hours, then drain; discard the liquid.

In a large pot, bring 10 cups water to a boil over medium-high heat. Add the bacon and beans and boil, uncovered, for 30 minutes. Add the ham, sausage, potatoes, zucchini, and cabbage. Bring to a boil and cook for 5 minutes. Add the onion, bell pepper, salt, pepper, cumin, and tomato sauce. Bring to a simmer and cook until the beans are soft (about 30 minutes).

If you're serving the soup in coconut shells, cut the coconuts in half through the equator—a cleaver works best—and discard the coconut water or save for another use. Spoon each serving of beans into half a coconut shell and serve alongside the ropa vieja (recipe follows).

(see photograph, top right)

Ropa Vieja

(Serves 6)

2½ pounds flank steak
3 green bell peppers, seeded
2 large onions
2 medium tomatoes
¼ cup olive oil
1 tablespoon fresh oregano
1 tablespoon salt
1 tablespoon granulated garlic
6 bay leaves
Pinch ground cumin
2 cups canned tomato sauce
½ cup ketchup
1 cup dry red wine

In a large pot, bring 12 cups water to a boil over medium-high heat. Place the beef in the water and bring back to a boil. Reduce the heat to medium-low and simmer, uncovered, for 1½ hours. Remove the beef from the liquid (pour the liquid into a bowl and set aside), and allow the beef to cool on a cutting board for 15 to 20 minutes. When it's cool, cut the beef into ½-inch strips and set aside.

Cut the bell peppers, onions, and tomatoes into long strips—the tomatoes can be cut into thicker wedges, as they will soften when cooked. Add the oil to the original pot and heat over medium-low heat. Add the peppers and onions and sauté for 3 to 5 minutes. Add the beef, the reserved cooking liquid, and all the remaining ingredients. Cook, uncovered, over medium-low heat, stirring occasionally, for 20 to 30 minutes. Serve hot.

Sublime Coconut Flan

(Serves 6)

2 cups sugar
6 large eggs
One 8-ounce can sweetened condensed milk
One 8-ounce can evaporated milk
One 8-ounce can unsweetened coconut milk
1 cup heavy cream
1 cup whole milk
1 tablespoon vanilla extract

Heat the sugar in a small nonstick pan over low heat, stirring continuously with a wooden spoon, until the sugar melts and becomes golden brown, 8 to 10 minutes. Pour the caramel into a 6 by 8-inch baking pan (the caramel should cover the bottom of the pan) or into 6 individual ramekins, then transfer to a hot-water bath to keep warm (see Note).

Preheat the oven to 350° F.

In a mixing bowl, beat the eggs until smooth. Whisking continuously, slowly add the condensed milk until incorporated, then add the evaporated milk, coconut milk, cream, milk, and vanilla. When well combined, pour the milk mixture into the baking dish or ramekins to form a layer on top of the caramel.

Transfer the baking dish or ramekins and the hot water bath to the oven. Bake for about 1 hour, just until the center of the flan sets, and refrigerate for at least 1 hour. Serve chilled, either straight from the baking dish or ramekins or unmolded onto chilled serving plates.

NOTE: To create a hot-water bath, arrange the baking dish or ramekins in a larger baking pan, then pour enough hot water into the larger pan to come halfway up the sides of the smaller ones.

February in New Orleans

a gothic saint valentine's day feast

February is a short but sweet month, full of snow days, comfort foods, and video rentals. The sun sets early, and for most, this is a time to stay bundled up inside (hoarding a pint of ice cream). Thank God Cupid swoops down to save us from this hibernating slump with Valentine's Day. This romantic holiday bursts onto the wintry landscape like an improvised saxophone solo. Bright red and pink boxes get wrapped up in cellophane, and sleek, long-stemmed roses wait for anxious suitors in shops and on street corners. Chocolate is everywhere, love songs are on the radio, and, as our hearts are lit with passion, the chill of February melts away. It's time to close the freezer door, open the lingerie drawer, and let the thawing begin.

What a perfect time to visit the steamiest town in the South (and my favorite), New Orleans. It's the birthplace of the very first cocktail (the Sazerac); the lusty vampires who populate Anne Rice's racy novels; and the hosts of our gothic Valentine's Day soiree, Caroline and Remy, who just got engaged. Caroline and Remy love music, they love food, they love New Orleans, and they're in love with each other.

THEY ASKED ME TO HELP THEM design a party with the energy and mischief of young love, the spice of Louisiana cuisine, and just a touch of the risqué. And with their endlessly romantic dispositions and flare for the dramatic, they insisted that I go as far as I wanted with the décor. "Don't hold back," Caroline said in a long drawl. "Make it wiiiild." Words I love to hear!

My first instinct was to forget the candy hearts. I would create a decadent, gothic dinner for lovers. (Think *Interview with the Vampire*, think black and white with drops of crimson—rose petals, succulent oysters, and bold red wines.) First, the big duh: the color red was a must. But in this day and age, red on Valentine's Day is about as wild as a twenty-pound house cat. So in amongst the red rose petals, along the border of the tablecloth, on the rim of the china, and even garnishing the food, I added splashes of hot pink and a bloodletting, vampish burgundy. That and the Sinfully Red martinis we planned to serve would put the alley back in any cat.

Once Caroline told me that six couples would attend the dinner to take in the magnificent dining room of their two-hundred-year-old home in the French Quarter, I considered her suggestion to go "wiiiild" a challenge. I became intoxicated with the idea of parties as a form of seduction, and with Valentine's Day as the excuse, this one had to be utterly irresistible. My plan for the table was an orgy of roses. I envisioned a quilt of rose petals covering a twenty-foot table; rose petals sculpted atop rich red velvet cake; and chocolate-dipped rose petals served as delicious dessert hors d'oeuvres on gold platters.

Who could resist this? And I haven't even mentioned the juicy bacon-wrapped filet mignon that would draw out the hedonist in each of the guests, igniting desire with every bite.

Of course, as much as all of this turned me on, there was still something missing. I needed my mischief, and she came to me in the form of iron candelabras dripping with red wax, shadows of candlelight flickering across the ceiling in evocative patterns, and the ultimate theater of the unknown, the Harlequin mask. Even a native New Orleanian like Caroline, who grew up steps from Bourbon Street, would be seduced by this spectacle. And as for her guests, I can only hope that none of them would be concerned about heart conditions—this party should get their blood pumping!

A Seductive Dinner, Louisiana Style

Christopher Wilson, head chef at the eponymous flagship of Emeril Lagasse's empire, helped me plan this sumptuous Valentine's menu. We worked from Emeril's standard (though always evolving) menu, and tweaked and combined a few signature dishes to get the balance of flavors just right. I have been a fan of Emeril's for years, and always try to squeeze in a good meal at his restaurant when I'm in New Orleans. I have a particular yen for the Tasso Creamed Spinach. How can such a simple side dish have such a strong and smoky punch?

I found out when Christopher Wilson and I sat down to plan Caroline and Remy's menu. Tasso, a highly seasoned and intensely flavored smoked pork, adds a terrific bang to many Louisiana dishes—from jambalaya to soups, pastas to seafood. Just a few diced cubes of tasso certainly kicked this spinach up a few notches.

But that was just one side dish in the bevy of delectable ingredients and flavors Christopher assembled for Saint Valentine's Day.

To start with, he chose Fresh Louisiana Oysters topped with Tangerines and Horse-radish Mignonette; then some juicy Bacon-Wrapped Filet Mignon with Crawfish Stew, the illustrious Tasso Creamed Spinach, and Herb-Roasted Potatoes. The finale: Red Velvet Cake with Creole Cream Cheese Coulis. If the succulent oysters don't make your heart race, the sinfully crimson cake will work its aphrodisiacal wonders in no time. I recommend serving this menu preplated for each guest, rather than from the table or a buffet. This is especially true if you are eating in the dining room (and dressed in velvet!).

Invitation for Romance

Who knows mischief better than a jester? To set the tone for the party, we intrigued the guests with a playful and suggestive invitation in the form of a jester's scroll. We wanted them to feel like kings and queens—and know that they were in for an unusual evening. A simple rhyme put a twist on the standard party information. Here's the one we made up; have fun concocting your own:

Come and toast Saint Valentine
With rosy cheeks and juicy wine
Don cap and cloak, we propose
Bring nothing please, but a single rose

Write or print the party information on a piece of high-quality cream-colored paper (use a paint pen or calligraphy set for a bold statement). Attach the paper to dowels with strong glue and let dry for twenty minutes. Glue a piece of red velvet to each dowel to cover where the paper attaches. To finish, tie gold and hot pink ribbons to both ends of the dowel. You can hand-deliver the invitations to your guests. Leave them on the front porch, with a doorman, or in the mailbox to add a little mystery.

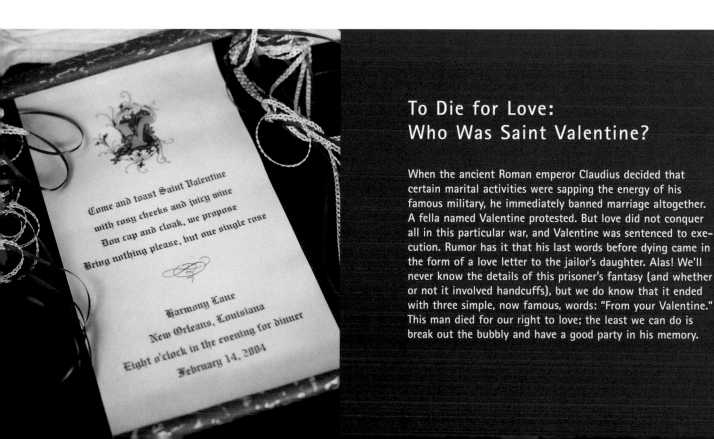

To Die for Love: Who Was Saint Valentine?

When the ancient Roman emperor Claudius decided that certain marital activities were sapping the energy of his famous military, he immediately banned marriage altogether. A fella named Valentine protested. But love did not conquer all in this particular war, and Valentine was sentenced to execution. Rumor has it that his last words before dying came in the form of a love letter to the jailor's daughter. Alas! We'll never know the details of this prisoner's fantasy (and whether or not it involved handcuffs), but we do know that it ended with three simple, now famous, words: "From your Valentine." This man died for our right to love; the least we can do is break out the bubbly and have a good party in his memory.

A Blood-Red Table

My truly decadent and devilish table was dressed up in burgundy-colored velvet and racy, hot pink silk. No matter what size your dining table, the key here is to make it a lavish surface for the display of your scattered rose petals, pink-trimmed china plates, chocolate desserts, and pretty flutes of champagne.

Find a tablecloth that falls all the way to the floor (I chose a burgundy velvet, though any heavy fabric in a shade of deep red or plum would work). Sew a 3- to 4-inch-wide hot pink fabric ribbon all around the trim of the cloth to create a vibrant border.

Chairs Spun of Gold

Rumpelstiltskin never spun as much gold as is displayed in these shimmering thrones. Organza adds immediate elegance to a room: It's the Grace Kelly of fabrics, and I love to use it whenever I can.

Select chairs with no arms, and wrap organza very tightly around the chair backs and the four legs until you've got three layers on each side. Attach the organza by either tying off the fabric in a knot or by fastening to the chair with rubber bands. Use no pins.

Passionate Place Settings

Though there are no heart-shaped objects on this table, the feeling is there with bright pink-trimmed plates with whimsical gold patterns, red champagne glasses, gold and clear wineglasses filled with burgundy wine, and red napkins bordered with hot pink edges (like the tablecloth) and embroidered with the word "passion." Medieval-looking gold flatware brings a bold confidence to these heart-thumping place settings.

A Flicker of Light

Any Valentine's Day dinner party will obviously have some candlelight, but if you want to really set a sexy and dramatic tone, use candlelight as the only light at your party. It achieves the kind of mischievous energy we're trying for, and, perhaps more importantly, it makes everyone look great! I opted for red candles in all shapes and sizes—from tall to tapered to thick pillars. Make sure your candles aren't scented or else your guests might end up wincing in an overwhelming cloud of cinnamon or rose perfume.

If you have a candelabra, this is the time to pull it out. What a perfect complement to a vampy Valentine's motif. Though simple iron candleholders are very effective in this setting, you can always add a few dangling red-hued crystals to contribute sparkle and a kind of boudoir feeling.

If you feel you need a touch of artificial light as well, try distributing small lamps around the edges of the room. Overhead lights tend to open the room up, detracting from the intimacy of this dining table.

Amaranths and Grapes

Nothing says Bacchanalian indulgence like cascading amaranths pouring from the table's edge. Try attaching these loose yet full red flowers to the corners of your table with safety pins (or florist pins). Sometimes called love-lies-bleeding, red cockscomb, or velvet flower, amaranths are rampant in tropical America and remind me so much of the Spanish moss hanging from the southern oaks. To push the envelope, try adding sugar-coated red grapes to the dangling bouquets.

- Spray the grapes with nontoxic glue.
- Roll them in white granulated sugar.
- Allow them to dry for 15 minutes.

Pick a Rose, Any Rose

For roses in the Valentine's Day color scheme of red and hot pink, use this guide to help you order from your florist.

Charlotte	bright red
Classy	bright red
Madame Delmar	burgundy
Black Magic	deep velvety burgundy
Nicole	deep red, white center
Red Magic spray roses	very full small red rose
Shocking Versilla	hot pink, large head
Hot Princess	deep pink
La Minuette	pink-edged, cream-colored blossom
Joy spray roses	hot pink small flowers
Pink Majolica	pale pink, very full cluster of small roses
Hocus Pocus	burgandy
Red Intuition	red with deep red stripes
Purple Cezanne	very saturated hot pink

Roses, Roses, Everywhere

I admit, a tablecloth of roses is a pretty indulgent fantasy, but if you're willing to go there, here's how to do it: Buy an abundance of roses (if you buy them two days early they will be fully blooming by the day of your affair). Carefully peel away the petals and scatter them over the dining table, sprinkling some full rose heads throughout.

You could scale this look down and simply decorate the outline of each plate or the perimeter of the table with rose petals. (Caution: roses stain! Cover the table with a fabric you are willing to part with after just one use.)

Salt and pepper servers are standard at any table, but how about making them out of rose heads? Simply carve out the midsections of two open roses and fill them with salt and pepper. Be sure to cut the rose where the head meets the stem, allowing the rose to sit upright on the table, and don't forget small spoons for serving. For the candlesticks, try placing rose petals around the base of the candle. It will create the illusion that the candle is coming right out of a rose.

Chocolate Roses

To test the boundaries of those at your party who claim to be true hedonists, try serving them chocolate-covered rose petals alongside sinfully indulgent chocolate fondue, chocolate cream Napoleons, chocolate covered strawberries, and red velvet cake, and see if they can handle the pleasure! These delectable floral desserts are also perfect for dressing up any winter dessert buffet, whether for Valentine's Day, Christmas, or New Year's Eve. They add an erotic touch to anything sweet. Try arranging them in small silver bowls, scattering them on a cake, or dropping them casually around a tray of ladyfingers.

- Add 3 ounces semisweet chocolate and 2 ounces milk chocolate to a double boiler. Heat until smooth (about 5 minutes), and remove from heat.
- Pinch off the bottom of the rose petal (the white tip)—it has a bitter taste.
- Using a spoon, drip the chocolate over the tips of your rose petals.
- Place the petals on parchment paper to cool for 45 minutes.

Come to the Masquerade

Entertaining in February in New Orleans just wouldn't be complete without a shout-out to the approaching Mardi Gras. There's no reason to go overboard, though—New Orleanians get their fair share of beads and feathers. For this mysterious party, I placed Harlequin masks at each place setting. If you have kids they can help you decorate simple masks with tissue, metallic sprinkles, and glossy gold, silver, and red paints. If you don't, you'll find these fanciful masks at most party supply stores, especially if you're in New Orleans.

Cocktail, Anyone?

When you're staring into the depths of your second or third martini, you might find yourself wondering where all this began. (I'm not talking about what some might call a serious drinking problem, but rather the invention of the very first cocktail.) The answer is New Orleans. Though folks have been fixing themselves drinks since the first fermented apple fell from the tree, it was the New Orleanian Antoine Peychaud who helped coin the term *cocktail*. When customers at his Royal Street drugstore praised his potent concoctions (made with bitters, cognac, and sometimes absinthe), they referred to them as *coquetiers*, the French word for the eggcup in which they were served. As time passed (and words became slurred), coquetier became *cocktail*, and we never went back.

The Modern Sazerac Cocktail

Peychaud used Sazerac cognac, absinthe, sugar, and his own bitters in his recipe. The drink later became known as the Sazerac Cocktail. You can order a Sazerac at the historic Fairmont Hotel on Baronne Street, but don't expect cognac or absinthe; this cocktail has gone through some serious renovations.

1 ounce Pernod
1 ounce Simple Syrup (recipe follows)
2 drops Peychaud bitters
1 ounce whiskey
Lemon twist

1. Swirl the Pernod and Simple Syrup in a chilled old fashioned glass.
2. Add the bitters and whiskey and garnish with the lemon twist.

NOTE: This drink is traditionally served neat.

Sinfully Red:
a perfect Saint Valentine cocktail

As your guests come in from the cold, you want them to be seduced by the aroma of roses, the vision of dripping, flickering candles, and the taste of a delicious cocktail. In this case, my strawberry and vodka concoction will begin the thawing process.

Lemon wedge
Red sugar (found in your grocery store's
cake-decorating section or made from
granulated sugar and red food coloring)
6 plump strawberries, fresh or frozen,
stems removed, sliced
3 tablespoons Simple Syrup (recipe follows)
3 ounces vodka, preferably Belvedere

1. Moisten the rim of a chilled martini glass with the lemon wedge and dip the rim into the red sugar.
2. Put five of the strawberries and the Simple Syrup in a blender and puree.
3. Put the strawberry liquid, vodka, and plenty of ice cubes in a cocktail shaker and shake vigorously.
4. Pour into the sugar-rimmed glass and garnish with the remaining sliced strawberry.

Simple Syrup

¼ cup sugar
¼ cup water

1. Combine the sugar and water in a small saucepan over medium heat and slowly bring it to a boil, stirring continuously until the sugar has dissolved.
2. Still stirring, let the mixture boil for 1 to 2 minutes, until a thick syrup is formed.
3. Remove from the heat, pour the syrup into a bottle or small decanter, and seal.

Love Is in the Air: My Favorite Love Songs

Though some stirring classical music (maybe a little Chopin) makes for a great introduction to this romantic soiree, have some CDs on hand for the after-dessert dancing. Don't be afraid to play on the emotions of your guests with a few old-school love songs. They won't be able to sit through this set:

"Love Is in the Air" (John Paul Young)
"Love Will Keep Us Together" (Captain and Tennille)
"I Will Always Love You" (Dolly Parton or Whitney Houston)
"Teenager in Love" (Dion and the Belmonts)
"Dedicated to the One I Love" (The Shirelles)
"Let's Fall in Love" (Diana Krall)
"You Were Meant for Me" (Jewel)
"The Way You Look Tonight" (Tony Bennett)
"To Make You Feel My Love" (Trisha Yearwood)
"When You Love Someone" (Bryan Adams)
"Let's Talk About Love" (Céline Dion)
"You're Still the One" (Shania Twain)

And to send them off, here's your DJ's grand finale: "You Send Me," performed by the most romantic crooner of them all, Sam Cooke.

Three E's

Essentials
- Rose Petals
- Chocolate Desserts
- Red Candles

Extras
- Pink- and Gold-Trimmed Glasses and Plates
- Draped Amaranths

Extravagances
- Iron Candelabra
- Organza-Wrapped Chairs
- Silk and Velvet Tablecloth

TUTERA TIPS

• To create a roses and candles centerpiece, take a plain square or round tile, cut rose heads flush at the base, and glue them around the perimeter of the tile. Place a red pillar candle in the center. The "fence" of rose heads prevents wax from dripping onto your cloth and looks great. Or for a more permanent centerpiece, use small silk rose heads.

• Use a small red or pink ceramic bowl filled with water, a few rose petals, and a votive candle in the center to accent the center of the table.

• Make your own pink and red colored glasses. Purchase basic glassware (with a beveled shape) and paint with translucent glass paint. Then add scroll accents with a gold-paint pen.

• Call your local florist and purchase discounted roses that are full-blown and about to be discarded. Scatter the petals on your table and the floor.

• Use old costume jewelry (from a brooch to a buckle) as a sparkly and inventive napkin tie.

• Glue small red spray roses around a simple napkin ring to create a bold, blood-red ring of roses.

• Pin pretty ribbon bows to the base of pillar candles, creating a lovely custom look.

• When blowing out a candle, hold one hand behind the candle to "catch" your breath. This helps prevent the melted wax from splattering.

• If you spill a little red wine on your clothing, use a little white wine to get it out. It works immediately, and you don't have to leave the table.

• Between the courses, offer rosewater towels to your guests. Simply soak red washcloths in rosewater for a few minutes. Refrigerate until needed, or microwave for 30 seconds before passing.

Au Revoir, New Orleans!

I was lucky enough to be a guest at Caroline and Remy's intimate gathering, and I have to admit that the evening did not go exactly as I had predicted. Don't get me wrong, I had intended to seduce them all along. But I never could have imagined the positively electric charge created by the collision of lovers and roses. Every guest who walked through the door did the same thing: a big kiss on each cheek for Caroline; a small sip (followed by one very big sip) of a Sinfully Red martini; and then straight to the roses. They scooped them up in their hands, let them fall through their fingers, smelled them, pinched them, tossed them, and ate them!

But it was at the very end of the night that this party took on a life of its own. After a dozen oysters, half a dozen nibbles on chocolate desserts, and eight slow dances with Caroline, Remy grabbed the candelabra, put on his mask, and threw open the French doors! Caroline knew just what to do. Without a moment's hesitation, she pulled up the bottom hem of her skirt, and swept the rose petals into its fold. The next thing you know all of the guests were out on the balcony showering themselves, and the people below, with rose petals as they danced to the music rising from the open saloon doors of the French Quarter.

It just goes to show that when you dress your party like the stage for an opera, you can count on your guests to set a passionate story in motion. As Sam Cooke's voice carried the couples through their last dance, the women's cheeks glowed with the color of the roses. Or were they blushing?

Courtesy of Christopher Wilson,
chef at Emeril's.

Fresh Louisiana Oysters
*with Tangerines and Horseradish Mignonette
on the Half Shell*

Bacon-Wrapped Filet Mignon
*with Crawfish Stew, Tasso Creamed Spinach,
and Herb-Roasted Potatoes*

Red Velvet Cake
with Creole Cream Cheese Coulis

Fresh Louisiana Oysters
*with Tangerines and Horseradish Mignonette
on the Half Shell*
(Serves 6)

*About 4 dozen well-chilled Louisiana or other fresh
oysters (8 oysters per guest), shucked and on the
half shell*
*About 2 dozen tangerines, peeled, all membranes
removed from the segments*
1 recipe Horseradish Mignonette (recipe follows)

Arrange the oysters on the half shell on serving plates and top
each oyster with 1 tangerine segment. Arrange the Pickled
Mirliton in fan shapes alongside the oysters. Spoon about 1
teaspoon of the Horseradish Mignonette over each oyster and
serve immediately.

Horseradish Mignonette
(Makes about 1 cup)

2 shallots, peeled and finely minced
*Grated zest and juice of 2 lemons (4 to 6 teaspoons
zest and about 6 tablespoons juice)*
3 tablespoons prepared horseradish
½ teaspoon Dijon mustard
½ teaspoon minced garlic
1 tablespoon champagne vinegar
6 tablespoons extra-virgin olive oil
2 tablespoons finely chopped fresh parsley
Salt and freshly ground pepper to taste

In a nonreactive bowl, whisk together the shallot, lemon zest
and juice, horseradish, mustard, garlic, and vinegar. Whisk in
the oil and parsley and season to taste with salt and pepper.
Cover and refrigerate for 12 hours or overnight. Before serving, bring the mignonette to room temperature and whisk
until well combined.

NOTE: A mignonette is a simple, classic French sauce most
often used to garnish raw oysters or clams. It always includes
cracked peppercorns and some sort of acid, such as vinegar or
lime or lemon juice, and may include other flavoring ingredients, like the minced shallots and horseradish in this recipe.

Bacon-Wrapped Filet Mignon

with Crawfish Stew, Tasso Creamed Spinach,
and Herb-Roasted Potatoes
(Serves 6)

FOR THE CRAWFISH STEW

¾ cup plus 3 tablespoons vegetable oil
1½ cups all-purpose flour
6 shallots, peeled and finely chopped
3 small carrots, peeled and finely chopped
1½ ribs celery, finely chopped
3 Roma or other plum tomatoes, diced
1½ tablespoons minced garlic
¾ cup red wine
6 cups beef broth, preferably homemade
3 bay leaves
3 sprigs fresh thyme
Salt and freshly ground pepper to taste
Creole seasoning powder, such as Emeril's Original
   Essence, to taste
12 ounces cooked and peeled crawfish tails
3 tablespoons unsalted butter
2¼ cups finely chopped scallions, green parts only

FOR THE FILETS MIGNONS

6 filets mignons (6 to 8 ounces each)
12 strips bacon
2 tablespoons Creole seasoning power, such as Emeril's
   Original Essence
3 tablespoons vegetable oil

TO SERVE

1 recipe Tasso Creamed Spinach (recipe follows)
1 recipe Herb-Roasted Potatoes (recipe follows)

Make the crawfish stew: In a skillet, heat the ³/₄ cup oil over
high heat until very hot. Add the flour and cook, stirring constantly with a wooden spoon, until the mixture turns a light
chocolate brown, 3 to 4 minutes. Remove the roux from the
heat, transfer to a heatproof bowl, and set aside to cool.

Heat 3 tablespoons of oil in a saucepan, then add the
shallots, carrots, celery, tomatoes, and garlic. Stirring frequently, cook over medium heat until the vegetables are soft,
about 4 minutes. Add the wine and cook until the liquid is
almost completely evaporated. Add the broth, bay leaves, and
thyme and bring to a simmer. Add the roux and whisk to combine. Season the sauce to taste with salt, pepper, and Creole
seasoning powder, then simmer the sauce for 8 to 10 minutes
over medium-low heat, or until the floury taste is gone. Set
the sauce aside.

Make the filets mignons: Wrap each filet with 2 strips of

the bacon and secure with 2 toothpicks or skewers. Season the filets on both sides with the Creole seasoning powder.

Preheat the oven to 400° F.

In each of 2 heavy, ovenproof skillets, heat 1½ tablespoons oil over medium-high heat until very hot. Add the filets and sear until golden brown and crusty, about 3 minutes on each side. Transfer the skillets to the oven and cook for about 15 minutes for medium-rare, or to desired degree of doneness.

Remove the skillets from the oven and transfer the filets mignons to serving plates, pouring the cooking fat and any accumulated juices into one of the skillets. Remove and discard the toothpicks.

Transfer the sauce to the skillet and reheat over low heat, stirring to combine with the fat and juices. Add the crawfish tails, butter, and scallions and cook for 1 to 2 minutes, until the crawfish are just heated through.

Spoon the crawfish stew over the filets and serve immediately, with the Tasso Creamed Spinach and Herb-Roasted Potatoes on the side.

Tasso Creamed Spinach
(Serves 6)

2 pounds fresh spinach (about 4½ bunches),
  well rinsed, tough stems removed
1 tablespoon vegetable oil
¾ cup (about 3 ounces) minced tasso (see Note)
1 teaspoon unsalted butter
6 tablespoons minced yellow onion
½ teaspoon minced garlic
4½ teaspoons all-purpose flour
1½ cups whole milk
¾ cup (about 6 ounces) grated Gouda cheese
¾ teaspoon salt
½ teaspoon Creole seasoning powder, such as Emeril's
  Original Essence

Bring a large pot of salted water to a boil. Add the spinach and blanch it for 10 seconds. Remove it with a slotted spoon and transfer it to a large bowl of ice water to stop the cooking. When the spinach is cool, remove it from the water and squeeze out any excess water with your hands. Chop the spinach and set aside.

Heat the oil in a skillet over medium heat, add the tasso, and fry until golden brown, about 2 minutes. Add the butter and when it's melted, add the onion and garlic. Cook until the vegetables are softened, about 1 minute. Add the flour, reduce the heat to low, and cook, stirring constantly with a wooden spoon, until a light roux forms, about 3 minutes. Add the milk and cook, stirring constantly, until the sauce thickens, about 4 minutes.

Remove from the heat and fold in the cheese, salt, and Creole seasoning powder. Add the chopped spinach and stir well. Serve hot.

NOTE: A Cajun specialty, tasso is a lean, richly seasoned chunk of cured pork or beef. Outside Louisiana, you can find it in some gourmet stores or by mail order.

Herb-Roasted Potatoes
(Serves 6)

2¼ pounds small Red Bliss potatoes, well scrubbed,
  quartered
3 tablespoons chopped assorted fresh herbs such as
  parsley, basil, thyme, rosemary, and chives
6 tablespoons extra-virgin olive oil
1½ teaspoons salt
¾ teaspoon freshly ground pepper

Preheat the oven to 350° F.

Combine all the ingredients in a large bowl and toss to mix well. Transfer the potato mixture to a roasting pan and roast until fork tender, about 30 minutes. Remove from the oven and serve immediately.

Red Velvet Cake

with Creole Cream Cheese Coulis

(Serves 8 to 12)

FOR THE CAKE
2½ cups sifted cake flour
2 teaspoons cocoa powder
1 teaspoon baking soda
1 teaspoon baking powder
1 teaspoon salt
1½ cups sugar
1 cup (2 sticks) unsalted butter, softened
2 large eggs
1 cup buttermilk
2 ounces (¼ cup) red food coloring
1 teaspoon distilled white vinegar
3 teaspoons vanilla extract
1 tablespoon vegetable oil
One 8-ounce package cream cheese, softened
1 pound confectioners' sugar
1 cup chopped pecans

FOR THE COULIS
4 ounces Creole cream cheese (see Note)
1 tablespoon honey
Grated zest and juice of 1 orange (about
  3 tablespoons zest and ⅓ cup juice)

Make the cake: Preheat the oven to 350° F, and grease and flour two 9-inch cake pans.

Sift together the flour, cocoa, baking soda, baking powder, and salt in a mixing bowl. Set aside.

In another mixing bowl, cream together the sugar and 1 stick of the butter. Add the eggs one at a time, beating well after each addition. A little at a time, alternately add the flour mixture and the buttermilk to the butter mixture, beating well after each addition. Add the food coloring, vinegar, 1 teaspoon of the vanilla, and the oil.

Divide the batter evenly between the two prepared cake pans and bake for 20 to 30 minutes, or until a cake tester comes out clean when inserted into the center of each cake. Remove from the oven, let cool for 5 to 10 minutes, and turn out onto a cooling rack.

While the cake is cooling, combine the cream cheese and the remaining 1 stick butter and cream together until smooth. Add the confectioners' sugar and cream together until light and fluffy. Add the remaining 2 teaspoons vanilla and mix well, then stir in the pecan pieces. When the cake is cool, smear the cream cheese frosting between the layers, stack them, and smear the frosting on the sides and top of the cake.

Make the coulis: Combine the Creole cream cheese, honey, and orange zest and juice in a small bowl and whisk together until smooth. Slice the cake and serve on individual plates, with the coulis either drizzled over the slices or spooned onto each plate.

NOTE: Creole cream cheese is a New Orleans specialty generally available outside Louisiana by mail order only. It's tart, with the texture of very thick sour cream. If you can't find Creole cream cheese, mix together 3 parts cream cheese with 1 part sour cream and use that instead.

March in Aspen

a ski brunch on the slopes

Breakfast is the most important meal of the day. Even if you failed P.E., chances are that some wholesome and responsible Phys Ed teacher drilled this nugget of truth into your mind before the last day of elementary school. Well, she was right. When you were eight years old, dashing out to the school bus with an English muffin in your hand, you knew she was right. And today, when you find yourself munching on a Carnation breakfast bar in the carpool lane at seven in the morning, you still know she was right. Unfortunately, most of us never sit down to enjoy the splendor of the morning and the sustenance of a good, homemade breakfast.

Luckily, some clever (and clearly overworked) genius created weekends, and in America, we put them to a good use: It's called brunch. Whether you like to spend the long morning enjoying a bottomless cup of coffee and a plate of "Moons over My Hammy" at Denny's, savoring a perfect rendering of eggs florentine in the dining room of the Four Seasons, or forking into a steaming plate of huevos rancheros at your favorite roadside diner, brunch is an essential weekend ritual. Of course, in the chilly winter months, it is a ritual best enjoyed in the comfort of your own home. This is especially true in March.

ALTHOUGH MARCH MEANS SPRING IS just
around the corner, there is still a brisk winter
bite in the morning air, and we haven't yet
fully awoken from our hibernating pace.
Good luck to anyone who tries to get me out
of my well-worn flannel pajamas on a cold
March morning! And the fleece slippers aren't
coming off, either, even with guests. After all,
you don't have to have earned a chef's
tocque to scramble eggs like a pro, and I find
that casual touches like this help everyone
feel free to lapse into the deep, slow and luxuriant rhythms of a good day off.

In the best of all possible worlds,
Sunday brunch isn't a day off work, but a
day off skiing the breathtaking slopes of
Aspen. That was exactly the case for myself
and five of my buddies on the last weekend
in March.

I was still nursing a few bruises from my spill on the Super Dragon Halfpipe, but I managed to hustle down to the kitchen before anyone else awoke. I have always believed that the best gift you can give your loved ones is a hearty, homey brunch. Try beckoning your friends from their peaceful winter slumber with the rich aroma of maple-scented oatmeal and hickory-smoked sausage links. It is a simple gesture that is full of love, and on a cold morning, it warms your very soul.

O f course, when I was eagerly planning the nuances of my brunch in the week that led up to it, there might have been a few instincts toward self-preservation mixed with all the feelings of love and largesse. If you've ever hurtled down Snowmass at warp-speed with only two ski lessons under your belt, you know the value of serene thoughts. For some, it's the sound of waves or Gregorian chant; for me, it was a thistle and birch centerpiece for the perfect breakfast table.

Aspen, I discovered, was full of inspiration for my holiday send-off celebration. The quaint, rustic charm of the shops and houses of Roaring Fork Valley, the spectacular sunsets melting into the mountains, and the fresh, newborn buds peeking out from snow-dusted branches in promise of springtime, all flooded my senses with images of nature's fragile beauty. This brunch would be a celebration of the cusp between winter and spring. Miniature bouquets of larkspur, daylilies, and cockscomb would burst forth from open eggshells perched in porcelain egg cups; a fluffy frittata of ratatouille and feta would go from the stove to the table in warm copper skillets; charger plates fashioned from thinly chopped birch logs would bring the great outdoors to the great indoors, bowls of fresh fruit and baskets of fresh, hot muffins and rolls would warm the air, and a winter throw would replace the standard tablecloth for that final cozy touch. This comforting winter repast, an ode to the ephemeral beauty of springtime in the mountains, would last well past ski season in the memory of my friends.

A Bountiful
Homemade Breakfast

There is only one way to describe the menu for this early spring brunch: down-home-away-from-home. It is both refined and comforting, fortifying and familiar, thanks to the genius of chef Todd Slossberg of the Hotel Jerome. Todd is one of Aspen's true culinary marvels, well known for lavishly nutritious brunches. He makes guests at his restaurant feel right at home while tucking into innovative, flavorful dishes, even when their ski togs bear the unmistakable creases of suitcase packing.

The menu Todd created for my brunch is a testament to his reputation, a fusion of high-energy foods made from top-notch ingredients. Mom might never think to finish off a brilliant hash of smoked Colorado ruby trout with poached eggs and an all-important smattering of fresh herbs, but then again, that's what made Todd's menu so exciting to my guests. And that was only the beginning: Whole Wheat–Granola Waffles with Fresh Pear Syrup wooed the sweet of tooth, while a gorgeously colorful Egg-White Frittata with Ratatouille, Feta, and Baby Spinach—which was served, to boot, with Fresh Tomato Relish—appealed to those of us who crave the glorious and the responsible in equal measure.

Of course, the entire menu is packed with whole grains, protein and vitamins, so all of us felt refreshed and energized enough to attack the slopes. No midmorning pancake-naps here! It was sporty, high-art comfort food, perfect for the mood of the occasion, and simple enough that I was able to prepare it for my friends myself. What could be more down-home than that?

The Breakfast Table

When entertaining in the morning hours, I recommend rousing your sleepy guests with a spread that captivates the senses. And when it comes to the visual and olfactory appeal of a well-laid breakfast table, no exceptions should be made. Crowd the table with delicious breakfast treats—even if your guests don't go back for multiple helpings from the jars of homemade jam, pots of creamy butter, piles of crisp toast, stacks of bacon, and pyramids of warm cornbread and sweet muffins, the mouthwatering aroma and vision of excess will surely make them feel like masters of the house (even if they didn't exactly master the slopes). After all, the beauty of a breakfast cornucopia is that it doesn't have to be complicated to be impressive. I like to think of it as the official meal of the American frontier, and if a guy working out of a covered wagon can pull off eggs, coffee, and corn cakes for a dozen hungry cowboys at dawn, you can pull off some spellbinding feats with a little help from the folks at Viking and Frigidaire. And there's no need to iron the linen napkins or polish the silver; morning in the mountains is a simple, cozy affair.

Of course, simple and cozy do not mean indelicate. The transition from slumber to wide-awake should be lovingly handled. Bring a little bedroom coziness to the breakfast table by substituting a winter throw for the average tablecloth. Keep the lighting warm and diffuse, and select napkins in rich, soothing tones such as plum, amber, and gold. I also like to bring a little of the woods to the table, and I couldn't resist creating a simple, earthy centerpiece from a few pretty birch logs and an armful of Aspen wildflowers. I even used thin rounds sliced from birch logs as charger plates, just to give the guy in the covered wagon a run for his money. These coarsely textured rounds complemented the centerpiece, but they also provided a necessary protective buffer between the table and the hot copper skillets used to serve individual frittatas to each guest. Together with yellow coffee mugs, a big pot of organic amber honey, and a copper decanter of freshly tree-tapped maple syrup, a comforting theme of golden warmth filled the breakfast room. But I couldn't forget approaching springtime: I brought out the cheerful Fiestaware, tied checked napkins with strong, flexible tulip leaves, and poured freshly squeezed OJ into wine-glasses decorated with hand-painted flowers. It may have been a revision of breakfast on the range, but Mother Nature was definitely dining with us.

Birch Tree Chargers

It's impossible to spend time in Aspen without falling in love with the quiet, simple beauty of the birch tree and its coarse, white bark. Birches are such a key part of the Aspen landscape (especially if you happen to be skiing toward one, the only time I was not happy to see a birch), that I knew from the beginning they would be an important part of my centerpiece. And I quickly discovered that the wood is terrifically practical: It's used to make everything from toys to toothpicks. Native Americans transformed birch into arrows, canoes, baby carriages, even snowshoes. The flexible wood absorbs stains easily and has a lovely wavy pattern. For winter fireside parties, (especially in Aspen, where you're guaranteed to find a pile of birch logs by the fireplace), why not saw off a few rounds for serving trays, charger plates, and cutting boards? If you've got the electric saw plugged in . . .

- Saw a log of birch wood into 1-inch sections. Get a seasoned woodcutter to help you with this, if you feel overwhelmed—but trust me, if you have the right tools it's as simple as slicing cheese!
- Remember that the chargers must be 2 inches larger in diameter than your main course plate; therefore, 12 inches should be a standard size for chargers.
- Add one coat of polyurethane to the charger. This will prevent the wood from flaking off. (Birch dries quickly and tends to flake.)

Colorado Wildflowers in Eggshell Bouquets

In about two months these mountains will be sparkling with a coat of Technicolor green and spotted from valley to peak with tiny explosions of Colorado wildflowers. And though far from the Austrian Alps, anyone who happens upon springtime in Aspen will surely throw up their arms and start singing just like Julie Andrews in *The Sound of Music*. March is a little early for this kind of spry outdoor outburst, but folks in Aspen can sense it's not far off. So why not fill cracked eggshells with miniature bouquets of the ravishing mountain flowers to come? I love delicate eggshell "vases," and encourage you to try making them yourself. Simply empty a raw egg by piercing a hole in both ends of the egg with a pin. Blow out the egg white and yoke into the sink. Crack the top off gently to create an opening for the flowers.

Intoxicant or Antioxidant?

When entertaining in the style of nature-loving Coloradans, be prepared to serve antioxidants as well as intoxicants. There are plenty of healthful perk-me-up (or chill-me-out) herbal elixirs to help you out. Start with smoothie basics, such as vanilla yogurt, frozen berries, bananas, and milk (soy, whole, or skim), and garnishes like fresh strawberries and mint. Then why not explore some of the smoothie supplements described below. They're fun to use even if you, as well as the FDA, are not sure of their benefits to your health.

Smoothie Supplements

These can be served in glass beakers (the kind you find in the science lab), or standard shot glasses. Either way, your guests will be on cloud nine.

Ginseng (Siberian): The root of the ginseng plant has a long history as a medicine in the Far East. It is said that ginseng increases one's energy and mental alertness.

Honey: An energy-giving food with carbohydrates, minerals, B complex, C, D, and E vitamins.

Flax Seed Oil: A rich source of essential fatty acids. Flax seed oil assists in reducing high cholesterol, relieving arthritis, and easing high blood pressure.

Rice Bran and Oat Bran: Great sources of water-soluble fiber, which helps to flush out your digestive tract. Bran has been shown to help reduce your total blood cholesterol level.

Vitamin C: Water-soluble vitamin believed to boost the body's immune system and provide resistance to colds, flu, and infections. Also benefits healthy blood flow and bone structure.

Kava: A worry-free way to forget the day. Fresh kava from Hawaii has the reputation of being a real stress reliever.

Lecithin: Supplemental lecithin is derived from soy beans. Found in every cell of the body, its primary function is to emulsify fats and cholesterol.

Cayenne Pepper: Oxygenates the bloodstream to help absorb and speed up the body's nutrient intake. High in vitamin A and minerals.

Spirulina (Super Green): Premium nutrient-rich super complex with Klamath Falls blue-green algae, spirulina, alfalfa, fruits, and vegetables. Shazzam!!

Aloe Vera: Used as a skin healer for burns, cuts, stings, bruises, sunburns, and skin irritations such as acne. Taking aloe vera internally may aid in the healing of stomach ulcers, torn muscle tissue, and other damaged internal areas.

St. John's Wort: Widely used as a stress reliever because of its ability to increase serotonin levels. Higher serotonin levels help control appetite.

Gingko Biloba: For the vitality and rejuvenation of the mind. Gingko extracts are widely taken for the treatment of age-related cognitive decline.

Brewers Yeast: The best natural source of B complex vitamins. It is extremely rich in protein and chromium, which is a key mineral in carbohydrate metabolism.

Bee Pollen: Contains eighteen amino acids, several minerals, enzymes used in digestion, and the B complex vitamins. Some individuals may have allergic reactions to bee pollen, and it should only be used in small amounts.

Three E's

Essentials
- Wildflowers
- Birch Logs
- Tablecloth Throw

Extras
- Eggshell Bouquets (see page 52)
- Self-Serve Smoothie Bar
- Yellow Fiestaware Bowls

Extravagances
- Birch Tree Chargers (see page 52)
- Individual Copper Pans
- Hand-Painted Orange Juice Glasses

TUTERA TIPS

- Serve four different juices in tall, glass pitchers lined up: What a colorful and simple display!

- Make the smoothie bar self-serve, with beakers full of supplements displayed on a glass (or Plexiglas) tray.

- Never wash an iron skillet with soap and water. Instead, let it cool and wipe it clean with a paper towel. If heavier cleaning is required, reseason your skillet by rubbing shortening over all surfaces (inside and out) and place it in a 200° F oven for at least one hour. Let cool, remove, and wipe down with paper towels.

- Make a one-pot herb garden for your kitchen window. Use an old strawberry pot to plant a variety of herbs in each of the holes. Make sure to plant the herbs that prefer wet soil toward the bottom.

- Keep your feet warm in the winter by adding $^1/_2$ teaspoon of cayenne pepper to the inside of your boots. Yes, it's true. The pepper actually stimulates heat sensations.

- When tomatoes are in season, cut into big chunks, remove seeds and liquid, and freeze in Ziploc bags. Then add to a blender with your favorite Bloody Mary ingredients, blend, and serve.

- Add diced chives, sun-dried tomatoes, or olives to low fat or regular cream cheese for a tasty bagel spread.

- To get the perfect fire going, start with very dry kindling. Build a progressive pyramid of dry firewood and light from the inside.

- March is a great time to start planning a small wildflower garden. Consult your local garden center for the appropriate varieties to plant in your region.

- A runner of wheat grass adds a great springtime look stretched down the center of your table. Be sure to first cover your table with plastic for protection and cut the wheat grass to size.

Adieu to Aspen

Suffice it to say that most of my friends didn't make it back to the slopes after our long and luxurious brunch. The jolt of ginseng in the smoothies was enough to power a quick snowball fight in the front yard, but we all kept our pajamas on under our snow pants; we knew how the rest of the morning would go. And it wasn't long before we were warm and cozy in the cabin once again. By the time the carafes of coffee were empty, we had all gathered on the cozy couches around the fire, and the only signs of the morning's feast were the smiles on our faces. But the sense of satisfaction and fullness I know each of us felt was the result

of more than a square meal. Later that day we would all have to part ways, catching planes heading back to the business of life. Winter would pass and the snow would melt, but like the bright wildflowers promised, spring would come soon, bringing something new to savor. And if only for one morning, we took the time to stop and enjoy the sensation of being together in the moment. *That's* why it's the most important meal of the day.

Some of us lounged around on a plush leather couch and nursed the remains of the coffee and smoothies. We joked about selling a video compilation of our week to the "Thrills and Spills" division of ESPN. Perhaps the unwritten rule about brunch is that nothing of importance should follow it.

March in Aspen
MENU

Courtesy of Todd Slossberg,
chef at the Hotel Jerome.

Colorado Smoked Ruby Trout
Flannel Hash with Eggs and Fresh Herbs

Whole Wheat–Granola Waffles
with Fresh Pear Syrup

Egg-White Frittata
*with Ratatouille, Feta, Baby Spinach,
and Fresh Tomato Relish*

High-Performance
Alpine Smoothie

Colorado Smoked Ruby Trout
Flannel Hash with Eggs and Fresh Herbs
(Serves 6)

*4 medium beets, preferably two red and two gold,
  roasted, peeled, and cut into 1¼-inch cubes
  (to yield 1½ cup)*
*3 large Yukon Gold potatoes, blanched until just
  cooked through, cut into ¼-inch cubes (to yield
  2 cups)*
1 medium white onion, minced
1 tablespoon fresh thyme
*½ tablespoon fresh summer savory or
  additional fresh thyme*
3 tablespoons clarified butter or vegetable oil
*1 pound smoked ruby trout, checked for bones
  and broken into coarse pieces (to yield 3 cups)*
1 tablespoon fresh Italian parsley, leaves only, chopped
1 tablespoon fresh chervil, chopped (optional)
Salt and freshly ground white pepper
*1 dozen large eggs, poached, fried, or scrambled
  to your preference*

In a mixing bowl, combine the beets, potatoes, onion, thyme, and savory, if using.

Heat the clarified butter in a large, well-seasoned cast-iron skillet (see Tutera Tips, page 54). Spread the beet mixture evenly on the bottom of the skillet, season with salt and pepper, and cook over medium heat until the vegetables are crisp on the bottom, 6 to 8 minutes.

Add the trout to the skillet and, using a spatula, flip the hash to the other side. It will break up a bit, but that's okay. Cook for 8 to 10 minutes more, until nicely browned.

Divide the hash among 6 warmed individual serving plates. Sprinkle with the parsley and the chervil, if using. Arrange 2 poached, fried, or scrambled eggs on top of each portion of hash and serve immediately.

Whole Wheat–Granola Waffles
with Fresh Pear Syrup
(Serves 6)

1¼ cups plain toasted granola
1½ cups milk
2 large eggs
½ cup (1 stick) butter, melted
1 cup whole wheat flour
½ cup all-purpose flour
1 tablespoon sugar
1 teaspoon cinnamon
1 tablespoon baking powder
½ teaspoon baking soda
¼ teaspoon salt
Vegetable-based cooking spray, for the waffle iron

FOR SERVING
1 recipe Fresh Pear Syrup (recipe follows)
Pear slices
¼ cup plain toasted granola (optional)
Sprigs of fresh mint

Combine the granola and the milk in a large mixing bowl. Add the eggs and butter and mix well.

In another mixing bowl, combine the whole wheat flour, all-purpose flour, sugar, cinnamon, baking powder, baking soda, and salt. Stir the dry ingredients into the wet ingredients and mix just until they are incorporated—a few lumps are fine.

Spray a preheated waffle iron with the cooking spray. For each waffle, pour in just enough batter to barely cover the grid; cook according to the waffle-iron manufacturer's instructions. Serve each waffle topped with Fresh Pear Syrup, pear slices, a sprinkle of granola if desired, and the fresh mint.

Fresh Pear Syrup

2 ripe pears, peeled, cored, and diced (to yield 1 cup)
1 cup maple syrup
1 vanilla bean

Puree ½ cup of the diced pears in a food processor or blender.

Heat the syrup in a saucepan over low to medium heat until it simmers. Add the pureed pears. Cut the vanilla bean in half, scrape the seeds into the pan, add the pods to the pan, and cook for 10 minutes, stirring to combine. Add the remaining ½ cup diced pears and cook to heat them through, about 5 minutes; remove the vanilla bean pods and discard. Serve warm.

Egg-White Frittata
with Ratatouille, Feta, Baby Spinach,
and Fresh Tomato Relish
(Serves 6 or more)

2 tablespoons olive oil
1½ cups Ratatouille (recipe follows)
2 cups egg whites (you may substitute whole eggs
  or use pasteurized egg products, if desired)
Salt and freshly ground pepper to taste
⅔ cup crumbled feta cheese
3 cloves garlic, thinly sliced
2 pounds baby spinach, well rinsed and patted dry
1 recipe Fresh Tomato Relish (recipe follows)

Preheat the oven to 350° F.

In a 10-inch nonstick ovenproof sauté pan, heat 1 tablespoon of the oil over medium heat. Add the Ratatouille and
warm it for a few minutes.

In a mixing bowl, whisk the egg whites for 1 minute, or
until fluffy but not stiff. Add them to the pan and stir to
evenly combine the eggs with the vegetables. Season with salt
and pepper. Cook until the bottom of the frittata starts to
brown and the sides start to pull away from the pan, 10 to
15 minutes.

Sprinkle the cheese on top of the frittata and place the
frittata in the oven until the top browns and the cheese
melts, about 15 minutes. Keep warm until ready to serve.

Heat the remaining 1 tablespoon oil in a large sauté pan
over medium heat; add the garlic and sauté until the garlic
turns a light golden color, 1 to 3 minutes. Turn the heat to
medium-low, add the spinach, season with salt and pepper,
and cook, stirring, until the spinach starts to wilt, 3 to
5 minutes.

Divide the spinach among 6 serving plates. Cut the frittata into 6 wedges and place a wedge on top of each serving
of spinach. Spoon the Tomato Relish around the edge of each
plate and serve immediately.

NOTE: Alternatively, you may prepare individual frittatas for
each of your guests and keep them warm in the oven until all
the frittatas are ready to be served.

Ratatouille

(Makes 4 to 6 cups)

¼ cup extra-virgin olive oil
1 medium eggplant, peeled and cut into ½-inch cubes
2 medium zucchini, scrubbed, seeded, and
cut into ½-inch cubes
1 large white onion, cut into thin strips
2 red bell peppers, seeded and cut into ½-inch cubes
1 tablespoon chopped garlic
3 medium tomatoes, peeled, seeded, and
chopped into ½-inch cubes
1 teaspoon fresh thyme
6 fresh basil leaves of equal size,
cut into chiffonade (see Note)
1 bay leaf
Salt and freshly ground pepper to taste

Heat a little of the oil (about 1 tablespoon) in a cast-iron skillet over high heat, add the eggplant, and sauté until lightly browned, 3 to 4 minutes. Transfer to a bowl and set aside.

Add another tablespoon of the oil to the skillet and sauté the zucchini until it's lightly browned, 3 to 4 minutes. Transfer the zucchini to the bowl with the sautéed eggplant.

Add the remaining oil to the skillet and sauté the onions. When the onions start to brown, 5 to 6 minutes, add the bell peppers and cook for 4 minutes, then add the garlic and cook for 1 minute more. Add the tomatoes and cook for 2 to 3 minutes, until most of the liquid has evaporated.

Return the sautéed eggplant and zucchini to the skillet, add the thyme, basil, and bay leaf, and toss to combine. Bring to a gentle simmer over low to medium heat and cook for about 20 minutes, stirring occasionally, until the vegetables are very soft.

Remove and discard the bay leaf, and season with salt and pepper. Serve warm. The ratatouille can be prepared the day before the party and refrigerated in an airtight container. Leftover ratatouille makes a good snack on flatbread or crackers.

NOTE: The key to creating chiffonade (thin strips or shreds) is to use a very sharp, thin-bladed knife. Stack the basil leaves flat on top of one another, roll them up like a carpet, and thinly slice—don't chop. When you unroll the basil, it will be in thin strips.

Fresh Tomato Relish

(Makes 1½ to 2 cups)

2 cups petite tomatoes, such as Sweet 100s,
cherry, teardrop, or grape tomatoes (see Note)
4 tablespoons extra-virgin olive oil
2 shallots, peeled and minced
2 teaspoons balsamic vinegar
Sea salt and freshly ground pepper

Wash and dry the tomatoes. Cut any tomato that's larger than bite-size in half.

Put the oil and shallots in a nonreactive bowl and whisk in the vinegar. Add the tomatoes and season to taste with sea salt and pepper. Let the relish sit for at least 30 minutes to allow the flavors to meld. Serve at room temperature.

NOTE: If you can't find petite tomatoes, use the best vine-ripened or beefsteak tomatoes you can find. Peel, seed, and dice the tomatoes, then continue with the recipe.

High-Performance Alpine Smoothie

(Makes 2 drinks)

1 large orange, peeled, all membranes
removed from sections
½ cup strawberries, fresh or frozen,
hulled and halved
1 whole banana, sliced and frozen
½ cup light vanilla soy milk, plus more if needed
½ cup low-fat yogurt
2 teaspoons protein powder
1 cup ice cubes, crushed
1 tablespoon orange juice concentrate

Combine all of the ingredients in a blender and blend well. Add more soy milk if the consistency is too thick. Pour into two Collins or highball glasses and serve.

April in Southern California

an impromptu wine country lunch and
a glamorous hollywood dinner

T. S. Eliot said, "April is the cruelest month." Obviously, he didn't spend his spring break sipping chenin blanc at a private vineyard in southern California, or hobnobbing with ingenues at a Spanish villa in the Hollywood Hills. Indeed, while the rest of the country is traipsing through puddles in their galoshes seven days a week, wondering if it's May yet, Californians are admiring fat, heavy vines of bougainvillea and tangled clusters of aloe vera; they are taking in the intoxicating aroma of night-blooming jasmine and honeysuckle; they are not waiting for May. In fact, for southern Californians, April might just be the kindest month (in a world of very kind months). The nights are still cool, and the midday sun hasn't reached summer levels of blazing, dry intensity. The valleys are still lush from the winter, the mornings are dewy, and those cleansing spring showers make even the famous cloud of smog over the Los Angeles basin seem more like a flattering soft-focus than the soup of carcinogens that it is.

Of course, the smog doesn't go on forever. If you travel just an hour outside of Los Angeles, you'll quickly realize that there are two sides to California. Far from the glamour of Sunset Boulevard, sun-baked coastal landscapes stretch from San Pedro to San Luis Obispo. Snow-capped mountains separate the breathtaking expanses of desert in the east from the eucalyptus-lined seaside roads to the west. Now, I myself have a lot of trouble choosing one over the other. Luckily, when I went to California last April, I got to have it all.

An Impromptu
Wine Country Lunch

Francis Ford Coppola got it right. Why
restrict yourself to the pleasures of
Hollywood when driving a few hours up or
down the coast lands you smack dab in the
middle of California's sun-kissed wine
country? All you have to do is survey the
gently sloping, golden hills of Napa,
Sonoma, or Ojai to understand what might
have lured the father of *The Godfather* out
of the movie studio and into the cellar. Of
course, you don't have to bottle the wine
to bottle up the experience of vineyard
lifestyle. As long as you have a wheel of
creamy Brie, a few ripe Bartlett pears, a
handful of wildflowers and a bottle of
something special, you have all the

elements. Life on the vineyard is, after all, simple. The garden, cellar, and kitchen are intimately connected; preparing a bite to eat is often a matter of selecting the right bottle of wine to go with the fresh bread, salami, and olives you picked up in town.

The locals in the vineyard towns here are deeply dedicated to cultivating what has become, over time, something like a North American annex of Italy. With more than 400,000 acres of wine grapes, 800 operating wineries, a cache of artisanal cheese and olive oil producers, and a formidable stash of chanterelle mushrooms, California definitely pulls its weight in the gourmet kitchen. But it's not just about the kitchen. It's about pacing your days according to the rhythms of nature, and eating and drinking straight from the earth. Once you've savored the simple, natural flavors captured in a salad of local goat cheese, fragile Black Mission figs, almonds, and mesclun, served with a hearty chunk of fresh ciabatta and a glass of chenin blanc, you'll wonder why there's a two-year wait list at The French Laundry.

In April I was lucky enough to find myself in Los Angeles working on a few projects, and I knew I couldn't bring myself to board a plane for the East Coast without a quick stop at my friend Toby's ranch near Ojai. As parties so often do in wine country, this one came together largely of its own accord. And, though I did have a hand in the table setting, the rest was up to Mother Nature.

On this perfect April afternoon, Toby had invited a few friends to stop by and raise a glass or two to the first spring blossoms. We worked together setting up our lunch in such an organic way, it seemed as though the olives poured themselves into bowls, the wine into glasses. The result was a table setting that perfectly mirrored the vineyard itself: The place mats were fashioned from grape leaves, the vases were recycled wine bottles, and the buffet tables were old oak wine barrels. Even the place card holders were made from corks! We picked tall grasses for lovely, breezy, fresh bouquets and filled baskets with apples and pears.

Between the guests' contributions, there were several different wines from six different California vineyards! And you can bet we sampled them all, perhaps breaking a few wine/food combination rules along the way. There was a spicy zinfandel from Sonoma, a crisp chenin blanc from Toby's own vineyard, a couple of smooth cabernets, and a zesty chardonnay macho enough to rival the flavor of Italian sausage and spicy dried tomatoes. As we uncorked one bottle after another, we feasted on crusty bread, California olive oils, balsamic vinegars, sliced prosciutto, garden tomatoes, black olives, slivers of Italian pecorino, and a dessert of rich mascarpone cheese topped with sliced figs and fresh mint. Thankfully, Ericka, my photographer, came along for the ride to document this impromptu April feast. She snapped away before we all sat down to devour our farm-grown treats, but I will always relish the memory of the table after our meal, adorned as it was with nature's decorations and the array of thoroughly enjoyed empty wine bottles.

The Ojai Table

Perhaps what I love most about the simple décor of vineyard living is that every element somehow relates to the process of harvesting and consuming delicious foods and wine. This characteristic makes the décor inherently transportable. Bottles of wine, bunches of freshly picked grasses and wildflowers, wedges of cheese and crusty bread served directly on a wood cutting board all add up to a celebration of function. Whenever I have to throw together a quick summer lunch on the patio or by the fire, I think back to my time in Ojai for inspiration.

A leafy place mat is a wonderful way to bring a touch of the great outdoors to a table without a big floral arrangement. All you need are six 8½ by 11-inch pieces of green construction paper; about twenty grape leaves, depending on their size, for each mat; and a glue stick. Begin by gluing leaves around the outer edges of the construction paper. Then work inward, creating subtle layers. When you reach the center, place one rounded leaf over the cluster of joining stems.

Wild Grasses

It may seem a little excessive to list the species of flora I found on a walk along Toby's driveway. Having said that, I have done more ridiculous things than order wild grasses from the florist! Sometimes there just isn't a long, grassy driveway outside your door. These are some tall, ornamental grasses you may want to order by name. If you decide to use a vase instead of a bottle, I recommend a tall and slender one that will keep the wispy reeds from drooping.

- Tapestry Millet
- Fountain Grass
- Setaria or Palm Grass
- Seeded Grass
- Fantail Greens
- Pampas Plume

When in Wine Country . . .

Wine connoisseurship is an ever-growing field, and there are a bevy of magazines and books that deliver tips on the latest, greatest grapes, best vintages, and noteworthy new labels to support. While I encourage the pursuit of connoisseurship, I also believe that a few basic principles about the complex world of wine-making and drinking go a long way. In this spirit, I've laid out what I consider the important guidelines for making the most of your California wines.

Getting the Temperature of Wine Just Right

This may seem unduly scientific, but the right temperature does make a difference! Room temperature is about 62–67° F (or warmer) so beginning with pinot noir, you can start considering some form of refrigeration (even if for fifteen minutes before serving).

Cabernet Sauvignon, Red Zinfandel, Vintage Port	62–67° F
Pinot Noir, Merlot, Shiraz, Syrah	58–63° F
Tawny Port	55–60° F
Chardonnay	50–55° F
Pinot Gris, Dessert Wines, Sparkling Wines	45–50° F
Chenin Blanc, Sauvignon Blanc	43–48° F

Bottle Sizes for Wine and Champagne Orders

- Split holds 375 milliliters or half a standard bottle
- Bottle holds 750 ml of wine
- Magnum holds same as 2 bottles, or 1.5 liters
- Double Magnum equals 4 bottles, or 3 liters
- Jeroboam equals 6 bottles of wine or 4 bottles of sparkling wine
- Imperial equals 8 bottles, or 6 liters
- Salmanzar equals 12 bottles (one case), or 9 liters
- Balthazar equals 16 bottles, or 12 liters
- Nebuchadnezzar holds same as 20 bottles, or 15 liters

Food and Wine Combining:
A Few Guidelines for Breaking the Rules

I always say, follow your instincts—and buy a decent bottle of wine! As far as food and wine matching go, there are certainly guidelines, but often a little straying from the rules can yield exciting results. The old rule about white wine with fish, chicken, and salads and red wine with meat, zesty pasta, and spicy foods made perfect sense when white wines were light and fruity and red wines were tannic and weighty. But today, when many California chardonnays are heavier and fuller-bodied than most California pinot noirs and even some cabernets, this trick doesn't always work. Here's a helpful list of wines, from lightest to weightiest, to help you match them with your food.

Selected dry and off-dry white wines, lightest to weightiest:

Soave, Orvieto, Pinot Grigio, Riesling
Muscadet, Champagne and other dry
    sparkling wines, Chenin Blanc
French Chablis and other unoaked Chardonnays
Sauvignon Blanc, White Bordeaux, White Burgundy
Pinot Gris (Alsace, Tokay), Gewürztraminer,
    Barrel-aged Chardonnay (United States, Australia)

Selected red wines, lightest to weightiest:

Valpolicella, Beaujolais, Dolcetto
Rioja, Pinot Noir
Burgundy, Barbera
Chianti Classico, Barbaresco
Barolo, Bordeaux
Merlot (United States), Zinfandel
Cabernet Sauvignon (United States, Australia)
Rhône, Syrah, Shiraz

Bottle It Up! Wine Bottles as Décor

Realizing that an empty wine bottle makes a great candleholder seems like a rite-of-passage for every college student. What a simple, bohemian solution for the fluorescent lights of dorm rooms! But even after college is well behind you, the beautiful swerve of a wine bottle is not just the subject of many a Cezanne masterpiece, it is a timeless classic; and, for me, the subject of many a striking centerpiece. Whether used as candlesticks, vases, or lamps, a row of wine bottles sets a rustic and romantic tone. So, before you take out the recycling from your last dinner party, consider these options:

• Insert a tall, tapered wax candle to create an elegant glass candlestick.

• Fill a few empty white wine bottles (the glass tends to be golden or pale-green hued) with water and plant clippings (such as ivy). Line them up on your kitchen window shelf and watch the sun beam through the bottles.

• You can make an oil lamp out of a bottle quite easily. You'll need a lamp-making kit (you can find them at craft stores) and an empty bottle. Basically, you fill the bottle with lamp oil and insert a wick and special bottle-stopper to seal the mouth of the bottle. But make sure the bottle is weighted and set in a steady location, so follow all warnings in the kit.

• If you're going to use a wine bottle as a vase, you'll need tall, fairly strong stemmed flowers or grasses (see page 64) so there's not a lot of flopping about.

My Favorite California Wines

There are so many exciting wines coming out of California, I can only advise that the best way to find your favorites is by trying them! Which is exactly how I came up with this list. The following California wines have been proven winners at many of my parties:

WHITE

Saddleback Pinot Grigio
Duckhorn Sauvignon Blanc
Vine Cliff Chardonnay

RED

Domaine Alfred Pinot Noir
Rosenblum Zinfandel (Ballentine Vineyard)
Hartwell Merlot
Snowden Cabernet
Frazier Cabernet
Rocking Horse Cabernet or Merlot
Shafer Syrah

Three E's

Essentials
- California Wild Grasses
- Empty Wine Bottle Vases
- Great California Wine!

Extras
- Cork Place Card Holders
- Grape Leaf Place Mats
- Wineglasses with Pretty Etched Patterns

Extravagances
- Chalk Hill 1999, Estate Vineyard Selection Chardonnay (an expensive California Wine)
- Antique Oak Barrel for Serving Food
- Wine Bottle Lamp

TUTERA TIPS

• Use corks as place card holders. Cut off a small piece of cork lengthwise, so that one side of the cork is now flat. On the curved side of the cork make a sliver in which to put a place card.

• Cover a wheelbarrow with a square of flat wood and decorate it with baskets of fresh fruit.

• Use a barrel as a drink and food bar (45-inch height is ideal for a cocktail or small buffet table).

• For a country lunch of hearty ingredients, try serving food on earth-toned ceramic and rattan chargers.

• Always hold your glass of wine by the stem. This keeps your body heat from affecting the temperature of the wine.

A Glamorous Hollywood Dinner

When we think of California today, we think of clean living. But this wasn't always the case. In Hollywood's golden era, crystal decanters filled with rye and scotch lined sideboards in offices, dining rooms, and living rooms. In *The Big Sleep,* Lauren Bacall's character even keeps one in her bedroom. And the beauty of it all was that nobody on the silver screen seemed to suffer. Drinking was not about getting drunk, it was about the rituals, the allure, the mystique. Of course, times have changed. Today we know our limits, and having a drink at noon is simply not a part of our culture.

But that doesn't mean we can't take a page from Hollywood's book of cocktail glamour. Whether lowball or highball, the accoutrements of cocktail culture can make an ordinary retro party feel double old-fashioned. And so, when my friend Eliza asked me to help her design an intimate supper for six friends that would evoke the dazzling past of Hollywood, I already had the concept in mind.

It couldn't have been more perfect. As a specialist in twentieth-century antiques, who supplies production designers and other industry-types with just the right authentic touches for their films and plays, Eliza deals in this very business of smoking jackets, Deco ashtrays, and bar carts. What fun! And when she told me her only requirement for the style of the party—that her love of all things vintage set the tone—I was thrilled. After speaking with Eliza about a few more specifics, I knew our stars were in alignment: the party would be held at her family's chic old Hollywood manse, high up in the hills of Los Feliz, a bona-fide glamour reserve.

Now, I have always believed that certain spaces have so much history that they speak to you, they tell you how to use them. And when they speak, it is essential that you listen; I have designed entire parties on the basis of a feeling I got from a room. And it was just that simple when I encountered Eliza's house. As I took in the elegant expanse of the Moorish ballroom, with its vaulted ceilings, high, slender windows, and dark wooden floors, which had no doubt enjoyed a lifetime of slow dances, images of the party to come unfolded before my eyes. I saw a romantic rendezvous beneath a canopy of honeysuckle and eucalyptus, and a languid waltz

to the theme from Casablanca. I saw great swags of silk and low light. I saw crystal decanters and a perfect arsenal of silver cocktail implements. With a little help from the silken curves of white calla lilies, the soft fall of a satin tablecloth, and a hint of soft-focus light from the café lamps, Eliza and her friends would not just live like stars for a night, they would feel like stars.

Old World Style, New World Palates

I know of only one chef in the Los Angeles area who could do justice to the Old-World Hollywood glamour of Eliza's get-together without smothering it in outmoded country-club pomp. Chef Josiah Citrin, of Santa Monica's award-winning Mélisse, imparts every classic European dish that leaves his kitchen with the distinct whimsy that befits his surfer lifestyle and SoCal aesthetic. For Eliza's dinner, he put together a menu that reimagined the simple, elegant flavors of Braised Short Ribs and Filet of Beef for a New Hollywood palate. The potato cakes that accompany his unusually subtle rendering of this exquisite cut of meat are spiked with barley and garnished with sweet roasted shallots. And to put a new shine on the salad course, he pairs Roasted Beets with Caramelized Endive and tops them off with Pistachio-Crusted Dates. There is no doubt in my mind that Citrin's signature Sherry Walnut Vinaigrette, which adds the final kiss of warm, bright flavor to this dish, will show up in your culinary dreams and in any available mason jars in your cupboard. (It's as simple to make as it is to devour.)

The crowning achievement of Citrin's menu is perhaps the miraculous ease with which these four-star delicacies can be whipped up in your own kitchen, as they were in Eliza's. The table-side service and Provençal landscape paintings that add to the refinement of the dining experience at Mélisse cannot be ordered as take-out, but the qualities and flavors of Citrin's recipes nevertheless evoked all of that elegance in Eliza's dining room. Her guests were enchanted by each bite of each formal course, but all bets were off when she placed before each of them a pristine slice of lemon curd tart. It was a refreshing reminder of the brisk spring days to come, and little did they know, it was the most effortless dish on the menu.

It's *the* Table in Town

The table setting was inspired by the blue tiles and rich camel-colored walls of the "fountain room," in which dinner was served. It may sound obvious, but as strong a statement as you may want to make for your dinner party, you must always pay attention to the details of your surroundings: the colors, the textures, and the light. I knew I wanted to let the hints of blue in the décor play off the indigo tiles of the fountain. So even though Eliza had a lot of materials from which to choose the fabric for the tablecloth, we chose Tiffany-blue sateen for the underlay and a stunning camel-colored duck-like fabric overlay with a white border. I wanted the cloth to fall like the swooping hem of a 1940s Hollywood gown. I had this tablecloth custom-cut for the occasion, and unless you are an avid seamstress, I would recommend against attempting to sew one together on your own. The difficulty arises in the rounded edges, which must be hemmed exactly right if there is to be a natural, flowing arc when the fabric falls. If you are not going to go with a custom job, a simple square overlay is the perfect substitute. Just let the sateen underlay spill and puddle onto the floor.

The chairs we used came straight from Eliza's dining room. This makes sense for such a small dinner party at home; I find it a bit over-the-top to rent chairs. To bring a little texture and continuity to the table, though, I draped a couple of faux-silver fox fur throws over two of the chairs. After all, a truly unique dinner party comes from the perfect marriage of the host's own style with the style of the party.

Silvery Hollywood Statement:
The Place Settings

Every cloud has a silver lining, and so do every plate and wineglass at this table. Sometimes silver looks best when it's used as a highlighter—much like the function of an eraser in a dark charcoal drawing. Silver trim brings up color, creates a sense of dimension, and adds to the formal composition of the table. Light blue and indigo plates, each with an ever-so-subtle silver trim, complemented a set of wineglasses with thick, ribbon-like silver borders. I perched the pearl-rimmed place cards on tiny, silver martini-shaped pedestals. They were like something out of a dollhouse! To complete the place setting, I simply placed one lovely calla lily across the napkin. Voilà!

A Bouquet of Lilies

Calla lilies to me are the movie stars of the flower world. Glamorous, pulled together, and perfectly proportioned, they come in white, burgundy, green, and other impressive, rich hues. For this retro affair, I placed one sleek Art Deco vase filled with white Casablanca lilies alone on a pedestal in the foyer. There, they made a lonely but dramatic statement. And it really set the tone for the night. I think just one similar flower arrangement can turn a great party into a work of art.

But I didn't stop there. I also made smaller bouquets of calla lilies, Casablanca lilies, tuberose, and white anthuriums. White anthuriums, like orchids, are grown in warm climates—I usually get mine from Maui. They may look delicate, but their flowers are tough to bruise and they generally last longer than any other cut flower. A vase with just a few anthuriums looks wonderful and will last you up to two weeks!

For the final touch, a low, round mahogany bowl filled with white calla lilies graced the center of the dining table. For a subtle, exotic touch, I weaved the buds together so that they formed the natural border of a dark wood bowl. To do so, I simply arranged them so that they overlapped side-by-side, curving around the edge of the bowl, and pinned them together with pearl-head pins. Perfection!

Ladies and Gentlemen . . .
Don Your Boutonnieres
and Nosegays

The term "boutonniere" is derived from the French word for the buttonhole on a lapel. The history of a groom decorating his coat with a bloom dates back centuries, and has held a variety of symbolic meanings over time. Now, unfortunately, the boutonniere seems to be an afterthought for most formal occasions. But at your party that can change! They are a lovely way to extend the theme of a party, in this case, pearls and calla lilies. At Eliza's party, each gentleman received a striking single calla lily boutonniere at the door, and the ladies received a small nosegay of miniature calla lilies. These gorgeous flourishes are very easy to make: Simply assemble a small bundle of flowers and wrap them with a little green floral tape. The women's nosegays are wrapped with white silk ribbon and pinned with pretty pearl pins.

When in Hollywood . . . Vintage Style

If Los Angeles is a mecca for vintage and thrift store devotees (and it is), then the monthly Pasadena Rose Bowl Flea Market is the ultimate pilgrimage. The true believers are there before seven o'clock in the morning to scour for rattan end tables, 1930s damask drapes, cowboy belt buckles, or those mod refrigerators from the 1960s that still have their revolving cheese trays. Like pretty much everything else in L.A., even the old is new here; virtually all of the antiques are late twentieth century. And the citizens of this kitsch-loving city take the business of retro very seriously.

Whether you're near a Burbank garage sale or not, there's always a thrift store (or vintage rental supply shop) nearby. And if you're hosting a glamorous cocktail party, chances are it will be just what the doctor ordered. For example, pearls are cheap, cheap, cheap! At Eliza's party, I used them as creative additions to the napkin ties, place cards, and café lampshades. Each napkin was embellished with a short strand of faux pearls I picked up from a neighborhood estate sale, adding texture and a whimsical touch to the table. But pearls are versatile, too: I trimmed small ecru place cards with faux pearls by simply gluing them around the border, and added them to the edges of lampshades. What a find!

Lights! Camera! Action!
Perfect Party Lighting

"I can't stand a naked light bulb, any more than I can a rude remark or a vulgar action," says Blanche DuBois in Tennessee Williams's *A Streetcar Named Desire*. Vivien Leigh, the star of the classic film version, would have looked nothing less than flawless in any light, even the cruel glare of a naked bulb. But her character, Blanche, certainly did have a point. No one likes to be looked upon with the scrutiny of a Beverly Hills facialist. There's a time for shedding light on the truth, and a time for letting the shadows fall where they may. And in the case of party lighting, the only thing any of your guests should see is themselves at their best.

Now, we can't rub Vaseline over our guests' spectacles, but we can use all the other tricks frequently employed by the Lifetime network. Rule number one: Pink, pink, pink! This warm hue blankets a room in an age-defying gold. To achieve this, you can buy soft bulbs (or in some party supply stores, even a pink bulb) and use yellow, gold, orange, or cream shades. Rule number two: Low wattage. If you're not going to blast the face with studio lights, go for the dimmer switch. Rule number three: low lights make rooms big. That's right, small lamps on tables and around the room add dimensions you never knew existed to almost any space. I also love the intimate, tailored look of small lamps set at each dining table. I use this technique all the time. For Eliza's dinner party, she broke out some blue café lampshades from the 1920s to go with the antique candlesticks. In place of these lamps, you could substitute a few silver or mahogany candlesticks with classic white tapered candles. And finally, rule number four: Fill the room with candles!

A Kiss Is Just A Kiss:
Glamorous Musical Selections

Eliza's guests were definitely in the mood to "play it again" when they heard the selection of music we picked especially for this occasion. We started with some upbeat soundtrack compilations including *Hollywood's Best: The Thirties* and *Hollywood's Best: The Forties* (both available on Rhino Records); then for dinner we were on to *Casablanca: The Original Soundtrack* and *Dr. Zhivago* (both are also on Rhino Records). To spark up after-dinner dancing, Eliza slipped on the Swingers soundtrack (there's also a Swingers Too soundtrack available, both on Hollywood Records). These are just suggestions. In the soundtrack section of your favorite music store, you'll no doubt be struck with nostalgia as you start flipping through discs. So buy your favorites, just keep in mind that the big show tunes and lyrical numbers are best for encouraging a spin on the dance floor after a cocktail or two.

Hollywood Cocktails

In her library of vintage gems, Eliza had a copy of a book called *Hollywood Cocktails* by Buzzo Cardozo, so we plucked a few cocktails for her party. These hip, retro cocktails will make your guests feel like they're lounging with Garbo and Fairbanks at the legendary Beverly Hills Hotel Bar.

Douglas Fairbanks Cocktail

2 ounces dry gin, preferably Plymouth brand
1 ounce French (dry) vermouth
Orange and lemon twists

1. Put the gin, vermouth, and plenty of ice cubes in a cocktail shaker.
2. Shake well and strain into a chilled cocktail glass.
3. Garnish with orange and lemon twists.

Garbo Gargle Cocktail

Dash white crème de menthe
1 ounce orange juice,
*   strained to remove pulp and seeds*
1 ounce grenadine
1 ounce French (dry) vermouth
1 ounce brandy
Splash port

1. Put the crème de menthe, orange juice, grenadine, vermouth, brandy, and plenty of ice cubes in a cocktail shaker.
2. Shake well and strain into a chilled martini glass.
3. Top with port.

Ginger Rogers Cocktail

1 ounce French (dry) vermouth
1 ounce dry gin
1 ounce apricot brandy
4 dashes fresh lemon juice

1. Put the vermouth, gin, apricot brandy, lemon juice, and plenty of ice cubes in a cocktail shaker.
2. Shake well and strain into a chilled cocktail glass.

Jean Harlow Cocktail

2 ounces rum, preferably Bacardi
2 ounces Italian (sweet) vermouth
Lemon twist or wedge

1. Put the rum, vermouth, and plenty of ice cubes in a cocktail shaker.
2. Shake well and strain into a chilled martini glass.
3. Garnish with the lemon twist or wedge.

Marlene Dietrich Cocktail

3 ounces Wineglass rye or Canadian whisky
2 dashes angostura bitters
2 dashes curaçao
Orange twist and wedge

1. Put the rye, bitters, curaçao, and plenty of ice cubes in a cocktail shaker.
2. Shake well and strain into a wineglass.
3. Serve with the orange twist and wedge.

Shirley Temple

Ginger ale
Dash grenadine

1. Fill a Collins glass with crushed ice and ginger ale.
2. Add the grenadine.

Will Rogers Cocktail

1 ounce orange juice, strained to remove pulp and seeds
2 ounces dry gin, preferably Plymouth
1 ounce French (dry) vermouth
4 dashes curaçao

1. Put all the ingredients and plenty of ice cubes in a cocktail shaker.
2. Shake well and strain into a chilled martini glass.

David's Favorite Escargots
(Serves 6)

½ cup (1 stick) unsalted butter, softened
2 teaspoons minced garlic
1 tablespoon finely chopped Italian parsley
1 tablespoon minced shallot
1 tablespoon freshly ground white pepper
1 teaspoon kosher salt, or more to taste
One 7-ounce can snails, rinsed
6 new potatoes large enough to contain
  the snails, scrubbed (optional)

Purée the butter, garlic, parsley, and shallot in a blender. Season with pepper and kosher salt.

Divide half the garlic butter among 12 sterilized snail shells or small ceramic containers. Stuff the shells with the snails (one snail per shell). Melt the remaining garlic butter in a small saucepan over low heat and drizzle over the escargots. Serve immediately.

Alternatively, preheat the oven to 400° F. Boil the new potatoes in salted water for 7 to 10 minutes until slightly soft. Drain the potatoes, cut them in half, and scoop out 1 table-spoon from each half to create holders for the snails. Divide half the garlic butter among the potato halves and stuff one snail into each slightly hollowed out skin. Bake for 10 minutes. Serve hot, with the remaining garlic butter melted and drizzled over the escargots.

Three E's

Essentials
• Calla Lilies
• Champagne
• Silver-Trimmed Glasses

Extras
• Silver-Trimmed China
• Boutonnieres and Nosegays
• A First Course of Fluted Asparagus

Extravagances
• Custom Deco-Inspired Tablecloth
• Escargots
• Imported White Anthuriums

TUTERA TIPS

• If you don't like escargot but love the butter sauce, try using the escargot sauce recipe on mussels instead.

• For an alternative to pomme frites (French Fries), substitute fried vegetables (carrots, celery, asparagus, or string beans) for the potatoes. Serve in paper cones for a first course or during cocktails.

• Glue ribbon or fringe to the edge of an ordinary lampshade. This is an easy and inexpensive way to dress up a lamp. Avoid hot glue, as it can melt from the heat of the light bulb.

• When pinning a boutonniere on a gentlemen's lapel, make sure to pin it on his left side, angled toward his left shoulder. This looks nice and won't get in his way during dancing.

• For unique napkin treatments, tie the gentlemens' white napkins with black bows and the ladies' napkins with strands of faux pearls.

California Dreaming . . . Heading Back East

As guests depart from this stylish evening, each received a special little Tiffany blue box wrapped with a camel–colored ribbon. When they opened it later, they discovered a small piece of costume jewelry: a glitzy rhinestone ring or elegant brooch for the ladies, and a handsome money clip for the gentlemen. These little accessories will come in handy whenever they feel the need to step out in Bogart (or Bergman) style, but more importantly they will remind Eliza's friends of their night as Hollywood royalty.

As for me, I always have a hard time leaving California. Long after I've left the Pacific time zone, I find myself listening to the Mamas and the Papas, longing for an In-N-Out burger, ordering my decaf latte with soymilk, and wearing flip-flops down Sixth Avenue. Then the reality sets in: I get "Monday, Monday" stuck in my head and realize that a quarter-inch of rubber sole just doesn't cut it on the sidewalks of New York. Slowly but surely, that Ojai tan fades and the city comes back into focus. I love visiting Toby, and I love the fanfare of L.A., but my everyday reality is more about amber waves of taxis than of grains. And when I'm hurtling down Fifth Avenue in one of those taxis, cell phone at the ready, the tranquil hills of Ojai and the secluded retreats of the Hollywood Hills are both literally and figuratively thousands of miles away from my mind.

No matter how much I revel in the energy of New York, there are very few doorman buildings that feature such amenities as remote hiking trails, gnarled cabernet vines, and grand Spanish ballrooms. But that doesn't mean that when I settle up with the cabbie at the end of my workday, I can't uncork a bottle of Toby's chenin blanc, swap my boots for a pair of flip-flops, and eat a light, refreshing salad of citrus, walnuts, and field greens for dinner. After all, the thing that ultimately helps me let go of my blissful days on the left coast is the inspiration that it gives me for the way I live my life every day. The casual opulence of Eliza's evening with friends, the easy camaraderie I felt with Toby as we raised a glass to the sun-soaked hills rolling for miles around us: These little moments illustrate how simple the pleasure of sharing a meal with friends can be.

April in Los Angeles
MENU

Courtesy of Josiah Citrin, chef and owner of Mélisse.

Roasted Beets with Caramelized Endive, *Pistachio-Crusted Dates, and Sherry-Walnut Vinaigrette*

Braised Short Ribs and Filet of Beef *with Potato Barley Cakes and Roasted Shallots*

Lemon Tarts with Fresh Raspberries

Roasted Beets with Caramelized Endive, *Pistachio-Crusted Dates, and Sherry-Walnut Vinaigrette*
(Serves 6)

6 small red beets
1½ tablespoons extra-virgin olive oil
Salt and freshly ground pepper to taste
4 Belgian endives
1½ tablespoons sugar
1½ tablespoons unsalted butter
Several drops fresh lemon juice
12 large dried dates
6 ounces Roquefort cheese
1 tablespoon heavy cream
½ cup unsalted pistachio nuts, finely chopped
2 bunches watercress, leaves only

FOR THE VINAIGRETTE
3 tablespoons sherry vinegar
3 tablespoons canola oil
3 tablespoons extra-virgin olive oil
3 tablespoons walnut oil
Salt and freshly ground pepper to taste
2 tablespoons chopped fresh chives

Preheat the oven to 375° F.

In a mixing bowl, toss the beets with the oil and season with salt and pepper. Wrap each of the beets in aluminum foil and place them in a baking dish with a little water so they won't burn. Roast the beets until they're tender when pierced with a knife, 45 to 50 minutes, adding more water to the dish as needed. Unwrap the beets, let them cool, then peel and cut each into 8 wedges. Set aside.

Remove and discard the ends and cores from the endives and separate the leaves. Slice the leaves lengthwise into thin strips. Put the sugar and butter in a sauté pan over medium-high heat and cook until the sugar is melted and a light caramel color. Add the endive and toss it in the butter mixture until it's well coated. Taking care that the butter doesn't burn, cook the endive until it's soft and golden, about 5 minutes. Season with salt and pepper and lemon juice. Transfer to a bowl and set aside.

Cut the dates in half lengthwise, discarding the pits. Soften the Roquefort cheese by incorporating the cream with a wooden spoon. Take about 1 tablespoon of the cheese mixture, roll it in the pistachios, and place it on top of a date half. Repeat until you've used all the cheese mixture and dates.

When it's almost serving time, preheat the oven to 375° F and, on separate trays, reheat the endive and the beets until they're hot, about 10 minutes. Prepare the sherry-walnut vinaigrette by putting all the ingredients except the chives in a jar with a tight-fitting lid and shaking well to combine.

In a nonreactive bowl, toss the hot beets with the vinaigrette, season with salt and pepper to taste, and let marinate in the bowl for about 2 minutes.

Remove the beets, reserving the vinaigrette in the bowl, and pinwheel 8 wedges on each of 6 serving plates. Divide the endive among the plates, placing it in the center of each beet pinwheel. Add the chives to the reserved vinaigrette and drizzle half of it over the beets. Top each mound of endive with 4 stuffed date halves. Toss the watercress with the remaining vinaigrette and place it on top of the dates. Serve immediately.

Braised Short Ribs and Filet of Beef *with Potato Barley Cakes and Roasted Shallots*

(Serves 6)

2¼ cups red wine
3 tablespoons vegetable oil
3 short ribs, trimmed of excess fat
Salt and freshly ground pepper to taste
Flour, for dusting
4 cloves garlic
½ small onion, peeled and cut into 1-inch pieces
1 small carrot, peeled and cut into 1-inch pieces
1 small rib celery, trimmed and cut into 1-inch pieces
1 small leek, cut into 1-inch pieces, then thoroughly
*   washed and drained*
1½ sprigs fresh thyme
4 sprigs fresh Italian parsley
1 bay leaf
1 scant tablespoon tomato paste
2¼ cups low-sodium beef or chicken stock,
*   preferably homemade*
6 tablespoons extra-virgin olive oil
12 shallots, unpeeled
6 filets mignons (4 ounces each)
1 recipe Potato Barley Cakes (page 80)

Preheat the oven to 350° F.

Pour the wine into a large saucepan, bring to a boil over medium heat, and cook until the wine is reduced by half. Remove from the heat and set aside.

Heat 2 tablespoons of the vegetable oil in a Dutch oven or flameproof casserole over medium-high heat. Season the ribs on both sides with salt and about 1 teaspoon pepper. Dust the ribs with flour, shaking off the excess. When the oil is hot, add the ribs to the pot and sear them until well browned, 4 to 5 minutes on each side.

Transfer the ribs to a plate and remove all but 1 tablespoon of the oil from the pot. Lower the heat to medium and toss in the garlic, onion, carrot, celery, leek, thyme, parsley, and bay leaf. Lightly brown the vegetables, stirring frequently,

5 to 7 minutes, then stir in the tomato paste and cook for 1 minute. Add the reduced wine and the stock, and return the browned ribs to the pot. Bring to a boil, then tightly cover the pot.

Transfer the pot to the oven and braise the ribs for 2½ hours, or until tender enough to pierce with a fork. Skim the fat from the surface every 30 minutes or so. Let cool, then chill the ribs in the braising liquid for 12 hours or overnight. The next day, scrape the fat from the surface and preheat the oven to 350° F again.

Heat the olive oil in a flameproof casserole over medium heat, add the shallots, and cook until the oil bubbles. Cover the casserole and transfer it to the oven. Roast the shallots for 30 to 40 minutes, until they are easily pierced by a knife. Remove the shallots from the oil and keep warm.

Cut the short ribs in half so that you have 6 pieces; return them to the braising liquid. Reheat the ribs in the oven, basting them often. Carefully transfer the ribs to a heated dish, cover, and keep warm. Strain the braising liquid through a fine-mesh sieve or chinois into a saucepan and cook at a simmer over medium heat until the liquid is reduced to about ³/₄ cup. Season with salt and pepper.

Increase the oven temperature to 425° F. Heat the remaining 1 tablespoon vegetable oil in an ovenproof skillet over medium-high heat. Season the filets mignons on both sides with salt and pepper, and then add them to the skillet. Cook for 2 minutes on each side, or until browned. Place the skillet in the oven and cook for 4 to 6 minutes more for medium-rare. Remove the filets from the oven, transfer to a plate, and let rest in a warm place for 5 minutes.

Before assembling the dish, be sure that all of the elements are warm, reheating if necessary. Remove the tough outer peels of the roasted shallots. Place a barley cake in the center of each of 6 warmed dinner plates and arrange a short rib and a filet on top of each cake. Place 2 shallots alongside and drizzle with the reduced cooking liquid.

Potato Barley Cakes
(Makes 6)

½ cup pearl barley, cooked (see Note)
3 large Yukon Gold potatoes (about 1½ pounds total), peeled, baked, and mashed
3 large eggs
Salt and freshly ground white pepper
½ cup all-purpose flour
1 cup panko or other coarse dry breadcrumbs (see Note)
Vegetable oil, for frying

Combine the barley, potatoes, and 1 of the eggs in a mixing bowl. Season with salt and white pepper to taste, then form the mixture into 6 patties about ³/₄ inch thick. Refrigerate until cold.

Put the flour, remaining eggs, and the panko on three separate dishes. Lightly beat the eggs. Dredge each barley cake in the flour, patting off any excess, then coat with the egg and dredge in the breadcrumbs. Dip into the eggs a second time, and then into the breadcrumbs. Return the cakes to the refrigerator.

Heat a large skillet over medium-high heat. Pour about ¼ inch of vegetable oil into the skillet. Add the barley cakes and cook until golden brown and hot, 2 to 3 minutes on each side. Serve warm.

NOTES: To cook the pearl barley, put ½ cup rinsed pearl barley in a saucepan with 1½ cups water or stock. Bring to a boil, then cover and reduce the heat to low; cook for about 30 minutes, until tender and fluffy and all the liquid has been absorbed.

Available at Asian markets, panko is breadcrumbs used for coating fried foods in Japanese cooking. Because the crumbs are coarser than those used in the United States, they create a nice crunchy crust.

Lemon Tarts *with Fresh Raspberries*

(Serves 6)

FOR THE PASTRY DOUGH
1 pound (4 sticks) unsalted butter, softened
¾ cup sugar
3 large egg yolks
3 tablespoons heavy cream
4½ cups all-purpose flour

FOR THE LEMON CURD
4 large eggs
4 large egg yolks
1 cup sugar
1 cup fresh lemon juice
½ cup (1 stick) plus 2 tablespoons
  unsalted butter, sliced

TO SERVE
Fresh raspberries

Make the pastry dough: Cream the butter and sugar in an electric mixer with a paddle attachment until light and fluffy. Add the egg yolks, one at a time, beating well after each addition. Add the cream and beat to combine, scraping the sides and bottom of the bowl thoroughly. Add the flour all at once and pulse the mixer until it is just barely incorporated. Wrap the dough in plastic wrap, flatten it into a disk, and refrigerate for at least 2 hours.

Preheat the oven to 350° F.

Roll out the dough until it's ¼ inch thick, and cut into six 6-inch circles. Use the circles to line 6 individual 4½-inch tart tins. Pierce the dough with a fork and bake until the tart shells are golden brown, 15 to 20 minutes.

Make the lemon curd: Whisk together the whole eggs and the egg yolks in a stainless steel bowl until smooth, then whisk in the sugar and then the lemon juice until well combined. Place the bowl over a pan of simmering water and cook, whisking occasionally, until the mixture is thick enough to slow the whisk's path, 20 to 30 minutes. Remove from the heat and add the butter, stirring to incorporate. Strain the lemon curd through a fine-mesh sieve, then divide it among the prebaked tart shells. Top with the fresh raspberries and refrigerate until cold.

When chilled, remove the tarts from the individual tins and serve.

May in Kansas City

an all-american memorial day cookout

April showers bring May flowers, and by the time Memorial Day rolls around, chances are you've paid your dues. The obligatory spring-cleaning has been done, you've devoted countless hours to your perennials, and you've tried on a thousand swimsuits (in fluorescent lighting, no less). The sun is finally out, and even better, you can wear your favorite white linen pants without making too big an impression. There's a buzz in the air all around you: The birds are tweeting, the bees are busy, and pop songs pour out of the open windows and sunroofs of every passing car. It all adds up to a delirious kind of music, the undeniable soundtrack of summer. And without a doubt, the ultimate expression of this season on the brink is the Great American Memorial Day Cookout.

Americans love their grills, and they will undoubtedly use them all summer. But absolutely nothing compares to the first hint of charcoal in the air that comes on Memorial Day weekend. It is the first day of the year when the basic human urge to grill makes even the fussiest of gourmands trade in their frisée and fennel for three pounds of chuck and a pack of Oscar Mayers.

O F COURSE, Memorial Day means more than opening day at the pool. It is also a time to honor the men and women who've fought to make America's way of life possible. And what better place to celebrate the selfless defenders of our country than in its heartland? This year, I'll hang my flag at a family-style fete in America's backyard, Kansas City, Kansas.

The postcards for sale at any roadside diner in the state will show you why my Memorial Day party had to be in Kansas: Golden fields of corn and sunflowers glow in the warm light, cattle graze for acres in every direction, and the sky is the bluest blue. The freshest ingredients grow in abundance, and their trip from the farm to the picnic table is just about as short as it gets.

But that's not all. One of the best things about being a party planner is having the opportunity to entertain with your dearest friends. Growing up in Westchester, New York, my best friend Allison and I spent countless lazy summers riding bikes, hanging out by the pool, and chasing after the ice-cream truck. Today Allison has a family of her own in Kansas, so when it came time to make plans for Memorial Day weekend, I picked up the phone and made her an offer she couldn't refuse: I would throw the ultimate Memorial Day cookout for her, her husband Kenny, and their eight-year-old daughter Jenny, and I'd do it all right there in their backyard. At first Allison laughed at the prospect ("You'll be lucky if you find two matching napkins in this house!"). Let's just say that she hasn't changed much since the bike-riding days. She'd much rather play a fierce game of dodge ball than experiment with pie recipes. But I told her not to worry. I had a vision of a true American holiday: gingham tablecloths, hot dogs and hamburgers on the grill, apple pies, gigantic wedges of watermelon, and pitchers of lemonade. A picnic table and a pioneering spirit were all we'd need to make this Memorial Day unforgettable.

Needless to say, this party was more down-home than the ones I usually throw. On the day before the party I found myself not in the foyer of some grand ballroom, but in the driveway of Kenny and Allison's charming colonial home on Montgomery Avenue. There would be no crystal chandeliers at this affair, but I was already looking forward to a party that would gain its sense of extravagance from the combination of simple, well-chosen elements and good company. The company was the easy part: A riot of pig-tailed girls flooded the front yard as we approached the house, and I instantly understood that Kenny, Allison, and their friends weren't the ones I had to impress; Jenny and her gang would be calling the shots. This presented a totally new entertaining challenge for me: Juggling bubble-blowers and a pin-the-tail-on-the-donkey blindfold with my usual set of cocktail shakers and simple white votives.

We spent the afternoon gathering ingredients, decorations, and supplies for the next day. Allison purchased apples for a bobbing contest, Kenny surveyed the sidewalk for the construction of a lemonade stand, and Jenny helped me roll knives and forks in red-and-white-checked napkins. As we all sat around telling stories, laughing, and assembling sunflowers in small terra-cotta pots, I found myself looking forward to Memorial Day with the contagious expectations of my very young guests. This would be the first party I'd ever host with a crayon sharpener in my arsenal of supplies. Toto, we're not at the Waldorf anymore!

Artful Backyard Cuisine

Bringing elegance to a big barbecue is not easy, but when I met Debbie Gold and Michael Smith, co-owners of 40 Sardines, Kansas City's preeminent gourmet establishment, I knew they were the culinary angels I was looking for to help bring my style of entertaining to a simple backyard picnic. I've included recipes for four different burgers, apple pies, and Mike's Red Hot Barbecue Sauce, but there's no reason to forgo a few sophisticated additions. And sophisticated additions are exactly what Debbie and Mike provided. They understood right away that this meal was all about color. The bright red Baby Summer Tomatoes, the bold Yellow Squash "Linguini," and the golden Sugar Baby Melon, all grilled to perfection, fit right in with the red-checkered tablecloth and the Crayola colors of this energetic early summer cookout.

Fresh ingredients are the cornerstones of Debbie and Mike's cuisine, and here they are showcased in a spectacular and creative manner: Rosemary-tinged shrimp supply buttery zucchini with the perfect zip, and Grilled Pineapple Skewers with Watermelon Salsa embody the savory punch of warm summer afternoons. The natural flavors dreamed up by these two epicureans are an expansion on the art of backyard cuisine, not a departure from it. Everyone will want to try a slice of Trudy's Apple-Lemon Pie, but who can resist Mike and Debbie's simple delicacies from the grill? From children to adults, this versatile menu will supply you with the most important ingredients of all for a Memorial Day picnic: Empty plates and wide grins.

A Picnic Invitation

For a simple family barbecue, a fun, creative invitation isn't out of place. Let's face it—we communicate via cell phone and e-mail all day long, so getting a little something in the mail is thrilling for anyone. My idea for this invitation was inspired by the classic icon of the American summer, the old-fashioned flyswatter. I used red ribbon to attach a colorful printed invitation to the handle of the flyswatter, making it both festive and functional. And even better, it perfectly introduces your guests to the playful spirit of this party: red, white, and fun-all-over!

- Purchase old-fashioned flyswatters at a hardware or houseware store.

- Personalize store-bought red-and-white-checked invitations with your own party information, or have invitations printed with a red-and-white-checked border. Remember to keep the font fun and casual, this isn't the time for fancy cursive. You could even get the kids to write them!

- Attach invitations to flyswatters with bright red ribbon.

- If this is a party for neighbors, simply drop these off on doorsteps; if sending across town, purchase mail tubes at a stationery or shipping store such as Mail Boxes Etc.

Red and White All Over:
Decorating a Memorial Day Backyard

Checks are very cute, very American, and very Dorothy. I say, for Memorial Day (not to mention Fourth of July, Labor Day, and any picnic in between) go for this classic look. And really go for it: Dress the table in a checked tablecloth, serve the food on checked plates, roll the silverware in checked napkins, even sport a red-checked apron to greet your guests and wear matching oven mitts when you guard the grill.

Spread Sunshine All Over the Place:
Working with Sunflowers

The sunflower is the Kansas state flower, and one of my all-time favorites. I love to see them poking up near the vineyards of northern California, or bunched in bins at flower stalls in Manhattan, or standing in tall rows across the windswept plains of the Midwest. They're so perky and cheerful (like smiley faces), and yet they're also dramatic and confident. Here's a bunch of ideas about what to do with them:

- Cut off the heads and display them down the middle of a table as a runner.
- Display half a dozen flowers, complete with their long stems, in tall clear vases on small tables surrounding the area of your party.
- Cut stems 6 inches from the heads and tie the stems together with florist wire, forming a dome of sunflower heads.
- Cut stems short and display in terra-cotta pots.
- For a larger party with a sunflower design to it, pin place cards to flower heads with pearl pins and arrange at a place card table.
- Fill a very large, shallow, yellow or ink-blue bowl with water and four floating sunflower heads.
- Pluck off the yellow sunflower petals and simply use the deep brown center of the flower for a modern look.

Things to Do with Terra-Cotta Pots

Terra-cotta pots are so affordable and endlessly useful. They have a classic shape and color that fits in with any backyard, and they can be used and reused until that horrible day when the cat knocks them off a ledge. I love to recycle them after a party by planting herbs and small flowers in them. For this barbecue I chose small ones to hold the silverware, crayons, and sunflowers, and large ones for rosé and champagne buckets. The remaining bases of the large pots made excellent charger plates and serving trays for the creative condiments.

Even Party Planners Eat on Paper Plates Sometimes

There's no reason to be afraid of paper plates at an outdoor lunch with kids: They're absolutely appropriate and convenient. Of course, as I suggested, if you add terra-cotta dishes as charger plates for red-and-white-checked paper plates you're adding just that much more charm (not to mention support for your dripping burger).

Homespun and Hardware Décor

Just because you buy the bulk of your party supplies from the local hardware store doesn't mean your party's going to look like the inside of your uncle's shed. Planning is required to get the décor to live up to your barbecue dreams, it's just that you're dealing with crayons and oven mitts, as opposed to ballroom chairs and champagne flutes. And besides, one trip to Home Depot and you'll understand why your uncle bought all that stuff! If you find yourself in the two-by-four aisle suddenly contemplating a new deck for the house, just remember your shopping list and keep walking.

Hardware Store Shopping List

- Terra-cotta pots and plates
- Barbecue tongs and spatula
- One big old barrel for the apple bobbing (you may need to ask your uncle for this one)
- Lighter fluid and safety matches or a fresh tank of propane
- A classic aluminum outdoor garbage can
- Mason jars to use for your homemade BBQ sauce and in place of water glasses
- A good twenty yards of white packing paper

Let's Get Grillin'

While there is no correct way to grill over charcoal, most professional chefs will tell you that a good grill makes all the difference. There are always new models on the market, but one thing I always suggest is to use a grill with a grill area of 18 inches. This improves the taste of your food by distributing more heat (and charcoal flavor) over more space. When it comes to arranging the coals, use long-handled tongs to spread them evenly in a single layer. Extend them about one inch beyond the area of the food. For indirect grilling, you need a disposable foil pan large enough to cover the surface below the food.

Flare-ups can wreck a great meal in seconds. Here's how to keep them under control: Lower the heat by raising the grill rack and spreading the coals so there is more space between them. Remove the meat and some of the coals or cover the grill. For excessive flare-ups, you may need to remove the meat from the grill and mist the flames with water from a spray bottle. Once the flames die down, you can return the food to the grill and resume grilling. Do not mist flare-ups on a gas grill. Simply close the lid and wait for the flare-up to die down.

If you are using a gas grill, make sure to clean it each time you use it. This simple maintenance will add years to the life of your grill and it will prevent flare-ups as the grill rack will be clean. Here's how to keep the gas grill clean: After every use, turn your grill on high for 10 to 15 minutes with the lid closed. Turn off the grill and let it cool slightly. Loosen the residue from the grill rack with a brass-bristle brush. This not only prevents sticking, but also helps to avoid flare-ups. When the grill is completely cool, wipe the inside and outside surfaces with a soft cloth and warm, soapy water. Rinse with clean water and wipe dry.

Mike's Red Hot BBQ Sauce

(Makes 1½ to 2 cups)

Bottle your homemade sauce, using my uncle's recipe, and cover the top with a square of red-and-white checked cloth tied neatly with kitchen twine. Don't forget to label your affectionately made concoction.

1 cup store-bought ketchup
2 tablespoons brown sugar or honey
1 teaspoon cayenne pepper, or less according
  to preference
½ teaspoon garlic powder, or 2 to 3 garlic
  cloves, minced
1 teaspoon salt
2 tablespoons Worcestershire sauce
¼ cup cider vinegar
½ teaspoon ground cilantro
½ teaspoon cumin
2 tablespoons olive oil
¼ teaspoon Liquid Smoke (see Note)

1. Combine all the ingredients, including the Liquid Smoke, in a saucepan. (For a different flavor, substitute mustard for the Worcestershire sauce and molasses for the brown sugar.)
2. Bring the mixture to a boil, then turn down the heat to low and simmer until the sauce is slightly thinner than ketchup.
3. Cool the sauce before transferring it to a mason jar, using a funnel.

NOTE: I prefer using charcoal with mesquite, pecan, or hickory wood chips, but Liquid Smoke works well if you're grilling without wood chips or making barbecue in the oven.

Ten Condiments Commandments

1. Don't be afraid of the family-sized Heinz. You may be tempted to display your ketchup in a tasteful ramekin with a small silver spoon, but unless the First Lady is coming over, your guests will be satisfied with the classic big squeeze.

2. Everyone has mustard issues. But in this case it is possible to please all of the people all of the time. Just present a good variety of mustards—the dazzling array of labels and bottle shapes will definitely cut the mustard!

3. Mayonnaise is technically a French sauce. Yes, it's salty, it's bad for you, it's the roadside diner dressing of choice, but find me one person in America who doesn't like even the tiniest schmeer on a sandwich. Always have my favorite—Hellman's Mayonnaise—out.

4. Signature Sauces. McDonald's has the special sauce, Newman has his "Own," every steak house has a "house dressing," and chances are you have a few tricks up your sleeve. Always offer your guests the option of the "house blend," whether it be teriyaki-based mustard, a variation on "French dressing," or a smoky barbecue sauce.

5. Relish is appropriately named. It's the final topper to any well-turned-out burger. Sweet relish, yellow relish, onion relish, any one of these will complement either a dog or a burger.

6. The Greeks, the Indians, the Lebanese, they all make this creamy condiment and so can you! Combine plain yogurt, finely chopped cucumber, garlic, and lemon juice for the perfect topping to the spiciest meat off the grill.

7. Salsa goes fast. Make lots.

8. Grilled onions for a grown-up burger. Since the grill is already tanked and ready to burn, why not grill some onions while you're at it?

9. BBQ sauce gives rise to great debate. No one will ever agree about how to make, cook, and use barbecue sauce and whether barbecue is just a sauce (many Americans consider barbecue a dish). For a burger cookout, serve homemade barbecue sauce, and offer small bottles of the stuff as parting gifts.

10. Thou shalt serve slaw. You might think of coleslaw as a side dish, but put it on your hot dog and you never will again.

Three E's

Essentials
- Terra-Cotta Pots for Flatware and Flowers
- Red-and-White-Checked Tablecloth and Napkins
- Sunflowers

Extras
- Terra-Cotta Pot Charger Plates
- Homemade BBQ Sauce Gifts
- Homemade Pickles

Extravagances
- Hey, this is a barbecue! Nothing too extravagant, please.

TUTERA TIPS

- Use terra-cotta pots for holding flatware wrapped in napkins.

- Serve corn with husks peeled halfway down and tied loosely with a bow of twine.

- Make a rustic wind chime from four miniature terra-cotta pots. Using two lengths of twine, attach the pots (upside down) and hang the two strands about 3 inches apart.

- If you happen to break a pot, use the broken pieces to block the hole of another pot, to prevent drainage.

- Terra-cotta pots make ideal candle or votive holders. Line your garden path with them; place them around the perimeter of the yard or along the edges of the porch.

- Use small terra-cotta pot saucers as coasters to match the terra-cotta charger plates.

- Try using aluminum foil as a scrub brush when cleaning your grill. Crush a large sheet of foil into a ball and scrub your grill back and forth. The results are astonishing.

- When the grill is still hot but dinner is over, put a roast on and let it slow cook as the embers cool. It's great for lunch the next day.

- For a larger outdoor barbecue, attach nametags (made from construction paper cut into the shape of hanging tee-shirts) to an old-fashioned clothesline with great big, wooden clothespins.

- Fill an open cooler with crushed ice; prop an array of opened pints of ice cream on the surface. Voilà! An opened Crayola box of ice cream!

Waving Goodbye to Kansas City

Perhaps the very best thing about the Memorial Day cookout is that it can last as long as you want it to. In Kenny and Allison's breezy backyard, the sparklers burned well past twilight, and the fading embers of charcoal glowed just brightly enough to light the way to the leftovers for one last nibble after nightfall. By the time a brave guest polished off the last slice of apple pie (and I'm not naming names, but a certain childhood friend of mine was seen with a smudge of whipped cream on her nose), evidence of a top-notch cookout was all around me: Kenny and Allison were still debating whether the Italian meatball burger or the classic cheeseburger was the perfect burger, the kids were working earnestly on a Crayola masterpiece at the picnic table, the gigantic jar of homemade dill pickles was completely empty, and the sweet, smoky aroma of grilled corn husks lingered in the air. My vision of the Great American Cookout in the heartland was complete.

Later, long after Jenny and her gang fell asleep sprawled out in the hammock with crayons still clutched in their hands, the rest of us took turns wishing on the stars. Maybe it was the fireflies we chased in the dark,

maybe it was the infectious joy of summer's arrival, but for just one day, we were all perfectly content with the simple things (like burgers) that make America the great (and tasty) place it is. We felt lucky for the beautiful day, lucky to be lounging around in the backyard like teenagers, and lucky for the pleasure of celebrating these things together. Parties are, after all, one of the most genuine expressions of a basic joy for life. And that's the best reason I can think of to put the utmost care into even the most casual get-together. Even Allison was made a believer in the value of a family get-together done right. As I packed up my bag of tricks for the flight home, she gave me a great big hug, thanked me profusely for the party, and quietly asked if I might leave the red-and-white gingham napkins behind; nothing could have made me happier.

May in Kansas City
MENU

Courtesy of Michael Smith and
Debbie Gold, co-owners of 40 Sardines.

**Baby Summer Tomatoes
and Sugar Baby Watermelon**
with Grilled Red Onion and Ancho Chiles

**Grilled Rosemary-Skewered
Shrimp** *with Zucchini and Yellow Squash
"Linguine"*

The Great American Hamburger

Pepper Burger

Turkey or Chicken Burger,
Caprese Style

Italian Burger

Grilled Pineapple Skewers
with Watermelon Salsa

Baby Summer Tomatoes and Sugar Baby Watermelon
with Grilled Red Onion and Ancho Chiles
(Serves 6)

¼ cup sherry vinegar
1 cup extra-virgin olive oil
Salt and freshly ground pepper to taste
6 ounces baby spinach, well rinsed
6 ounces baby arugula, well rinsed
*1½ large red onions, trimmed, cut into ¼-inch thick
  slices, and grilled*
*1½ pints petite tomatoes, such as teardrop or
  currant tomatoes, halved*
*¾ small Sugar Baby watermelon or seedless yellow
  or red watermelon (about ½ pound), rind removed,
  cut into ½-inch cubes*
*3 ancho chiles, soaked in warm water for 5 minutes,
  seeded, and cut into thin strips*

In a nonreactive bowl, whisk together the vinegar and oil to
create a vinaigrette. Season with salt and pepper.

In another mixing bowl, combine the spinach and arugula with the grilled red onions, tomatoes, melon, and chiles.
Drizzle with about 6 tablespoons of the vinaigrette, taking
care not to overdress, and gently toss the salad. Safe the leftover vinaigrette for another use.

Arrange the salad on 6 individual serving plates, making
sure each serving includes some onion, tomatoes, and melon
along with the greens.

Grilled Rosemary-Skewered Shrimp *with Zucchini and Yellow Squash "Linguine"*
(Serves 6)

Six 12-inch-long sprigs fresh rosemary
36 jumbo shrimp, shell on
Salt and freshly ground pepper to taste
3 zucchini
3 yellow squash
¾ pound dried linguine
7 tablespoons extra-virgin olive oil
3 cloves garlic, peeled and thinly sliced
1½ cups picholine olives or other tiny black olives

Skewer 6 shrimp on each rosemary sprig. Season with salt and pepper and set aside.

Using a mandoline, cut the zucchini and yellow squash into long thin strands that resemble linguine. Shave each vegetable until the seeds appear, then turn 90 degrees and repeat.

Cook the pasta in boiling salted water until al dente. Drain in a colander, transfer to a bowl, and toss with 2 tablespoons of the oil to keep it from sticking. Cover the bowl and keep warm.

Cook the shrimp skewers on a hot grill for about 4 minutes on each side, until the shrimp are lightly charred, firm, and pink. Set aside.

Heat 5 tablespoons of the oil in a large skillet over medium-high heat. Add the garlic and let sizzle for 30 seconds. Add the zucchini and squash "linguine" and cook for 1 minute, stirring often. Add the olives and the pasta, tossing to combine them with the rest of the ingredients.

Transfer the linguine mixture to a serving platter and place the shrimp skewers on top. Serve immediately.

The Great American Hamburger
(Serves 6)

The burgers that follow are my own favorite recipes.

2 pounds freshly ground chuck steak
Salt and freshly ground pepper to taste
6 slices Vermont white cheddar cheese
6 fresh onion rolls
6 tablespoons spicy brown mustard
6 slices red onion
6 slices smoked bacon, cooked until crisp
1 large bunch arugula, well rinsed and patted dry

Prepare a charcoal fire or preheat a gas or stovetop grill to medium-high.

Season the steak with salt and pepper. Form patties, $^1/_3$ pound each and about $^3/_4$-inch thick. (Hamburgers cook too fast if they are too thin and take too long to cook if they're too thick.)

Place the patties on the grill. Cook them for about 3 minutes per side for a medium-rare burger, or to desired degree of doneness.

When the hamburger is almost cooked, place a slice of cheese on top and let it melt. Cut the onion rolls in half and place them on the grill to lightly toast.

To build the burger, spread 1 tablespoon of the mustard on the bottom half of the bun and place the hamburger patty on top. Add a slice of onion next, followed by the bacon, then the arugula, and, finally, the top of the bun.

Pepper Burger

(Serves 6)

1½ pounds ground beef
1½ tablespoons cayenne pepper
Freshly ground black pepper to taste
1½ tablespoons ground cumin
1½ tablespoons brandy
Salt to taste
6 sesame buns

Prepare a charcoal fire or preheat a gas or stovetop grill to medium-high.

Mix the beef, cayenne pepper, black pepper, cumin, brandy, and salt and form the mixture into patties, ¼ pound each. Don't handle the meat too much, or the burger will be tough. Season each patty with additional black pepper just before grilling.

Place the patties on the grill. Cook them for about 3 minutes per side for a medium-rare burger, or to desired degree of doneness. Toast the buns on the grill.

Serve the burgers on the buns with pickles and your favorite toppings and condiments.

Turkey or Chicken Burger,
Caprese Style
(Serves 6)

1½ pounds ground turkey or chicken
3 tablespoons chopped fresh basil
1½ tablespoons freshly ground white pepper
Juice of 1½ limes (about 2½ tablespoons)
Salt and lemon pepper to taste
6 whole wheat buns
1 large bunch arugula, well rinsed and patted dry
2 fresh mozzarella balls (6 ounces each), sliced
2 large beefsteak tomatoes, sliced
Balsamic vinegar
Olive oil

Prepare a charcoal fire or preheat a gas or stovetop grill to medium-high.

Mix the turkey, basil, white pepper, lime juice, and salt together and form the mixture into patties, ¼ pound each. Season the patties with lemon pepper just before grilling.

Put the patties on the grill. Cook them all the way through, 3 to 4 minutes. Turkey burgers should never be served rare. Toast the buns on the grill.

Serve the turkey burgers on the buns with arugula leaves, mozzarella, tomatoes, and drizzles of vinegar and oil.

Italian Burger

(Serves 6)

1½ pounds spicy Italian sausage, casings removed
⅓ cup fresh basil leaves, chopped
3 tablespoons oregano, chopped
1½ tablespoons Dijon mustard, plus more for serving
1½ tablespoons tomato paste
Salt and freshly ground pepper to taste
6 fresh onion rolls
2 fresh mozzarella balls (6 ounces each), sliced ¼-inch thick
Marinara sauce

Prepare a charcoal fire or preheat a gas or stovetop grill to medium-high.

Mix together the sausage, basil, oregano, mustard, tomato paste, and salt and pepper and form the mixture into patties, ¼ pound each.

Put the patties on the grill. Cook until well done, 3 to 5 minutes per side. Toast the rolls on the grill.

Serve the burgers on the rolls with the mozzarella, marinara sauce, and additional mustard.

Grilled Pineapple Skewers
with Watermelon Salsa
(Serves 6)

FOR THE VANILLA SYRUP
½ cup sugar
¼ vanilla bean

FOR THE SKEWERS
1 large fresh pineapple, trimmed, cored,
and cut into bite-size cubes

FOR THE WATERMELON SALSA
3 cups diced watermelon
1½ cups red seedless grapes, cut into quarters
1½ tablespoons fresh minced basil
1½ tablespoons fresh finely chopped mint
3 tablespoons Leonardi saba (see Note),
or good-quality balsamic vinegar

TO SERVE
Sprigs of fresh basil and mint

Soak 12 bamboo skewers in water for at least 1 hour.

In a small nonreactive saucepan, combine the sugar and ½ cup water. Scrape the seeds from the vanilla bean, add the seeds and the pods to the pan, and bring to a boil. Remove from the heat and refrigerate until cold.

Prepare a charcoal fire or preheat a gas or stovetop grill to medium-high.

In a mixing bowl, combine the watermelon, grapes, vanilla syrup, basil, mint, and saba; toss gently and set aside.

Put 4 cubes of pineapple on each skewer and put the skewers on the grill. Cook until the pineapple is charred and heated through, about 2 minutes on each side.

Ladle the watermelon salsa into the center of a serving platter. Arrange the pineapple skewers on top and garnish with the sprigs of basil and mint. The contrast of warm pineapple and cool salsa will be exciting.

NOTE: Leonardi saba is made from cooked grape must aged in barrels. Besides adding a sweet flavor to desserts and other dishes, it can be added to sparkling water and served as an apéritif. It's available at gourmet food stores or by mail order.

Trudy's Apple-Lemon Pie
(Serves 8)

FOR THE PASTRY DOUGH
2 cups all-purpose flour
1 teaspoon salt
⅔ cup plus 2 tablespoons shortening
6 tablespoons ice water

FOR THE FILLING (SEE NOTE)
1 large egg
1 cup sugar
1 tablespoon all-purpose flour
¼ teaspoon salt
Juice of 1 large lemon (about 4 tablespoons)
¼ cup unsalted butter, softened
3 large apples, peeled, cored, and cut into ½-inch
pieces

Make the pastry dough: In a mixing bowl, combine the flour and salt. Add the shortening and water and mix with your hands until well combined; the dough should form a ball without being too sticky. If it's too wet, sprinkle with flour. If it's too dry, add a little more water.

Divide the dough into 2 balls, flatten into disks, and wrap in plastic wrap. Refrigerate for at least 30 minutes.

Preheat the oven to 350° F.

Make the filling: Use an electric mixer to beat the egg, in a mixing bowl, until it's thick and light. In another bowl, mix together the sugar, flour, and salt. Add the dry mixture to the egg and beat until combined. Add the lemon juice and mix well, then add the butter and beat until combined. Add the apples and mix well with a wooden spoon.

On a lightly floured surface, roll out each disk of dough into a circle—they should be large enough to hang slightly over the edges of a 9-inch pie pan. Line the pan with one circle of dough and pour the filling into the pie shell.

To create a basket-weave top, cut the other disk of dough into 1-inch-wide strips. Crisscross the strips on top of the pie, weaving them over and under each other. Trim the edges with a pastry cutter and use a spoon or fork to seal the strips to the edge of the bottom crust.

Bake the pie for about 45 minutes, until the top is brown and the filling is bubbling. Serve, warm or chilled.

NOTE: This filling is too runny to be used with a store-bought pie crust.

June in Santa Fe

a summer solstice celebration

Santa Fe has inspired too many great artists to name in one place, from Georgia O'Keeffe to D. H. Lawrence. And though I don't presume to put myself in their company, the sun-baked vistas of red earth and blue sky have definitely inspired my work, too. By work, of course, I mean life. Like Georgia O'Keeffe, who spent half the year in New York and half in New Mexico, and who loved them both equally, I like to have my earth tones and taxis, too. I lived in Santa Fe for long enough to know just what serenity really means, and I try to visit whenever I need to rediscover that meaning. But when the last-minute flight to Albuquerque is not in the cards, I don't worry too much because I know that when I walk into my Manhattan loft, I'm as good as there. The dining room is painted in the rich, earthy tones of a Taos mesa at sunset: burnt orange, ochre, and pale blue set my soul at ease. I have designed little pockets of my personal refuge, my home, as love notes to Santa Fe; this is how much the spirit of New Mexico means to me.

Like any place, Santa Fe has its eccentricities. And before I start rhapsodizing about the cool, clean lines of adobe architecture, the play of light against the deep red canyons, and the explosive colors of dusk, there's a matter that must be addressed.

THIS IS NEW AGE COUNTRY. Sure, there's a great tradition of East Coast intellectuals wagon-training into Santa Fe for the summer opera series or the June gallery openings, but there's a kaftan for every poet, a healing stone for every sculptor. This makes some people uncomfortable. But I'm here to reassure you that after you've hiked an ancient Indian trail to the towering heights of a plateau and surveyed the kind of art that no human hands could make—the natural art composed of nothing but time and land, you might be ready to pop in that soundscape CD your massage therapist recommended. Take my word for it: New Agers connect this landscape with spirituality for a reason, and even if you're a hardened cynic, giving in to the accoutrements of Santa Fe (yes, this includes wind chimes)

can make you feel this connection even when you're miles away in body, if not in spirit.

Luckily, I was in Santa Fe in both spirit and body for the gallery opening and summer solstice celebration of my painter friend Iola. I love working with artists and gallery owners for any occasion. They usually offer small jobs, but to work with people so in tune with the design of their environment is a deep pleasure and a great inspiration; I always jump at the chance. And the chance to work with Iola was a great one. With a baby due in October, a brand new art studio off historic Canyon Road, and a wonderful exhibition of new paintings to celebrate, the air was electric with creative exultation. What a great energy to tap into! I knew this party would be extra special.

As I got to know Iola I got to know what she wanted, and little by little, I figured out how to translate this beautiful moment in her life into a party. Having studied in Paris, lived for years in Spain, and recently relocated to New Mexico, she is the quintessential cosmopolite. She loves French food and café culture, and relishes Santa Fe because it gives her that same sense of a vibrant art community, but in a spectacular natural habitat. Of course for all this cultural experience, she's deeply invested in the spirituality of the Southwest, in those things you cannot put into words, as Georgia O'Keeffe often said.

Iola makes every apparent contradiction—culture and nature, community and solitude, experience and innocence—feel instead like seamless parts of an organic whole. That's exactly what makes Santa Fe a great place, and if I had anything to say about it, that's what would make this party great, too. French cuisine and the fresh local flavors of avocados and chiles would sit side by side; formal place settings would adorn a low, makeshift table covered with a paint-splattered drop cloth and surrounded by cushions; natural New Age soundscapes would counterpoint the conversational buzz between the artists. Thank God it was the longest day of the year; we'd need all that time to enjoy every little bit.

A Soothing, Sophisticated Meal

I live in Santa Fe for a month every summer to soak in the landscape, enjoy the gallery scene and sample as many of the phenomenal regional restaurants as I possibly can. Over the years I have followed chef Mark Kiffin's career in the kitchen, from the famous Santa Fe–based Coyote Café to his consulting work for the immensely popular Washington, D.C.–based restaurant Red Sage, to the opening of his latest, and perhaps greatest, Santa Fe enterprise, The Compound. Here, Mark blends the best of French culinary traditions with his flair for the unusual and exotic. He takes advantage of local ingredients and techniques, but mostly he delivers mouthwatering French dishes that would make any bona-fide Cordon-Bleu chef proud. And though I whipped up my favorite guacamole and margaritas to start off the night at Iola's, I knew that a really spectacular French meal would perfectly complement the chic and sophisticated back-to-nature tone of the gathering.

Mark loves to teach, write books, and speak on the subject of food, so when I approached him to consider designing an appropriate menu for Iola, he leapt into action and created three simple, sensual recipes. The first course, a Brie Soup topped with Toasted Almonds, set the mood of this meal: creative and comforting. Next up, we served Slow-Baked Salmon with Chardonnay-Butter Sauce and watched Iola's guests unravel from the aroma of the sauce alone. For dessert, Iola brought out a piping-hot Roasted Rhubarb and Strawberry Rustica in a Santa Fe clay baking dish and served healthy-sized spoonfuls onto earthenware plates for each guest. After dinner, guests were simply glowing from the warm, soothing atmosphere of the room as well as the deliriously tasty French meal.

Summoning the Spirit of the Summer Solstice

The summer solstice is a magical time no matter where you are: In Sweden, locals celebrate a sun-soaked midnight hour with feasts and dancing. In Ireland, folks light bonfires on hilltops. Some believe that June 21st—with the sun at its strongest—is deeply connected with creativity and fertility and can be an especially good day for a wedding, a marriage proposal, or a baby blessing. I can't think of a better day for Iola's double celebration of her new paintings on the walls and her new baby on the way. Iola seemed to effortlessly connect with the spirit of summer solstice.

As Iola and I worked together to transform her studio into a party atmosphere, I realized that what we were capturing was the sensation of flow: between inside and outside, between art and life, between work and play. The party moved from the adobe patio to the indoor studio, making the entrance less a dividing line than a connecting line. If you don't have a breezy, open studio on Canyon Road, you can still create a flowing atmosphere at your summer solstice celebration:

- Hang wood chimes above doorways and in windows.
- Draw attention to windows by lining windowsills with votive candles and pots of spiky, aromatic rosemary plants.
- Hang billowing cotton curtains in wide doorways.
- Direct small fans (on low settings) toward ferns and other leafy houseplants, to create subtle movements and breeze.
- Use the same plants you have in the garden as centerpieces and decorations for the inside of your house.

The Artist's Table

I decided to use a low, draped table for this casual affair, and to forgo the chairs. The idea of Iola and her guests sitting around on plump cushions was too hard to resist after learning what a die-hard yoga fan she was. And besides, I knew she would appreciate how the low lines of this set-up can relax the environment of a party, without making it any less luxuriant or elegant—if it's good enough for a sultan. . . .

This look was made-to-order for Iola's bohemian rhapsody, but it can also be adapted very well for a variety of other occasions, from a bridal shower, to tea with friends, to a Sunday evening of Scrabble and salsa for two. And the best thing of all might be how easy it is to make happen. Use a sturdy round tabletop; the heavier it is, the more stable it will be. Support the tabletop with sturdy crates of either metal or wood; again, the heavier the better. Make sure that the crates are positioned as close to the edges of the table as possible for added stability. Chartreuse silk cushions add texture and compliment the color of the aloe—and the guacamole!

Drop-Cloth Tablecloth

What could be more perfect for a celebration of creativity than using a painter's drop cloth to dress the table? Iola made it easy: Even her "mess" was a work of art. But you don't have to be Jackson Pollock to make this look happen at your house (and that's probably best for everyone involved—believe me, I saw the movie). A few basic tools are all you need.

- Lay a neutral drop cloth on the ground in a well-ventilated area, such as an open garage, backyard, or patio.
- Choose three to four earth-tone paints (more than that will muddy easily); Iola's cloth was sky blue, light green, orange, and light brown.
- Mix equal parts of water-based or acrylic paints and water in mason jars. If the mixture is thicker than whole milk, add more water until it thins.
- Dip a 4-inch-wide paintbrush (an old one works great) into the paint, tap it on the side of the can and sling it in fast, jerking motions (like cracking a whip...). Oh, and make sure you aren't wearing your new Prada get-up.
- Allow to dry for 2 to 4 hours or overnight.

An Organic Centerpiece

As much as I love the music of Earth, Wind and Fire, they were not the inspiration for my centerpiece. But that's not to say that earth, wind, and fire were not all represented in my small, spiky, and yet soothing table arrangement. Santa Fe is just one of those places where you can find yourself completely mesmerized by the shifting patterns of clouds, or the dazzling erosion patterns in a massive red mesa. I felt compelled, as Iola does with her art, to capture the beauty of these simple organic building blocks in every detail of this table setting. I began with a shallow, wide silver bowl and a twisty aloe vera plant. Then I surrounded it with lava rocks (earth), tiny faux butterflies and turquoise stones (wind), and beeswax candles and small Mexican orange blossoms (fire). The result was a work of living art.

Elemental Color Scheme:
Earth, Sky, Water

I am very serious about colors. I am also very emotional about colors. And according to color theorists, there's a scientific reason for this. Though I don't know exactly how the perfect shade of twilight blue triggers a flood of endorphins, I do know that a harmonious color scheme induces in me a sense of happiness and well-being. If you want to tinker with the moods of your guests and affect the emotional undercurrents at your Santa Fe–styled party, here is a color chart to guide you:

- Red is the color of energy, rejuvenation, strength, power, love, passion, courage, vitality, and self-confidence.
- Yellow is the color of wisdom, clarity, intelligence, confidence, and learning.
- Blue is the color of knowledge, health, wisdom, protection, inspiration, calm, confidence, creativity, and communication.
- Indigo is the color of intuition, mysticism, and understanding.
- Brown represents stability, earthiness, and reliability.

Aromatherapy

Just as colors and sounds trigger strong emotional responses, smells have wonderful (or not so wonderful) effects on our moods. I like to remind my clients that a guest's first impression of a party is often what hits their nose, not their eyes or ears! Just as the sweet scent of cider and cinnamon can set the perfect tone for a holiday cocktail party—even before guests take off their coats—the soothing aromas of peppermint, rosemary, or citrus really invigorate a long, lazy summer afternoon. So, as you're agonizing over matching napkins at your local mall, remember to pick up a pot of fresh rosemary and rub some peppermint oil on your temples.

Aromatherapy, the practice of using pleasant smells to positively affect one's mood, is a wonderful subliminal touch to a hip, Santa Fe artist's soiree. Iola has an explosive herb and flower garden, filled with chamomile, rose, lavender, daisy, carnation, and lily. Use these scents in bunches, in sachets, in tea, in elixirs and bath tonics. For summer months, try candles that have been infused with the essence of lavender, gardenia, citrus, or eucalyptus. Blooming rosemary or a bowl of dried lavender are lovely touches for small tables around the house. And these simple fragrances do more than make you feel relaxed, they have medicinal rewards, too. So, if your guests find that they sleep well after your party, you'll know it was those tiny bunches of lavender!

- Jasmine oil eases depression.

- Eucalyptus and wintergreen oils relieve congestion.

- Lavender oil reduces anxiety and improves sleep.

- Lemon, orange, and other citrus oils improve mood and increase mental alertness.

- Peppermint oil relieves nausea and aids digestion.

- Rosemary oil assists in pain relief and muscle relaxation.

New Age Music Never Hurt Anyone

When I suggest playing "New Age" music to certain clients, they sometimes wince and recoil. "New Age!" they exclaim, "Is that cult music?" My response is always, "Trust me, this is the kind of music that blends so well with an environment, guests will hardly notice it (except for the fact that they are suddenly relaxed and laughing)." Whatever your feeling is about the genre, New Age music happens to be very soothing and relaxing. And it's not necessarily the cliché of harp music overlaying the sounds of a trickling creek! I find that a good selection is always welcome.

If you're looking for pure, unadulterated, relaxing guitar, try Will Ackerman. Ackerman created the popular New Age Windham Hill label, and plays intimate acoustic guitar at its finest. In fact, anything put out on the Windham Hill label is a lovely choice for a relaxing affair. Try George Winston's albums named for the four seasons—they're addictive. There are four CDs I have next to my stereo, in my car, and on my Sunday afternoon chill-out play list: Enya (*Paint the Sky with Stars*), Enigma (*LSD: Love, Sensuality, Devotion*), a Pure Moods compilation (various artists), and the Instrumental Moods compilation (various artists). They're all classics of a modern stripe.

Perfect Margarita

Salted or not salted, frozen or on the rocks, margaritas
are a Southwestern staple. I always say the key to a univer-
sally loved margarita is top-shelf tequila and lots of fresh
limes!

1 ounce fresh lime juice
   (from kaffir limes, if you can find them)
1 teaspoon superfine sugar
1 ounce Grand Marnier
2 ounces high-quality tequila
   (I recommend Petron Silver)
Lime wedges
Margarita salt or coarse kosher salt

1. Stir the lime juice and sugar together in a cocktail
   shaker until the sugar is dissolved.
2. Add the Grand Marnier and tequila, along with
   plenty of cracked ice, and shake well.
3. Rub a lime wedge around the rim of a lowball or
   margarita glass and dip it in salt.
4. Pour the contents of the shaker into the glass and
   (including the ice) garnish with a lime wedge.

Straight-Up Good Guacamole
(Serves 6)

A great guacamole is not just a condiment; it's a way of life.
Here is a recipe I learned from hanging around red-tiled
kitchen counters in Santa Fe watching locals whip up a
quick snack with a mortar, pestle, and a few ripe avocados.

4 large ripe avocados, peeled and pitted
½ cup chopped red onion
½ cup chopped seeded Roma or other plum tomatoes
½ cup coarsely chopped fresh cilantro
Juice of 1 large lime (about 2½ tablespoons)
1 to 2 cloves garlic, finely minced
1 to 2 teaspoons seeded and finely
   chopped serrano chiles
1 teaspoon cayenne pepper (optional)
Salt to taste

TO SERVE
White and blue corn chips
Sour cream

1. Using a large mortar and pestle, mash the avocados to
   desired consistency (I prefer chunky).
2. Add the rest of the ingredients and mix until well combined.
3. Serve immediately, with corn chips and sour cream.

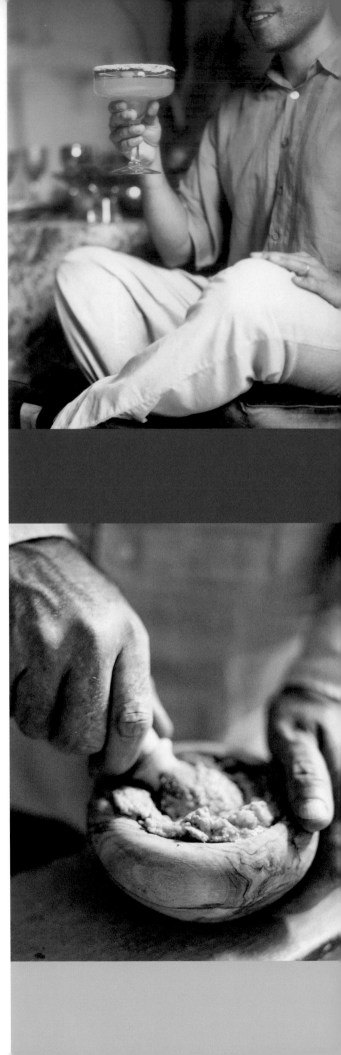

Three E's

Essentials
- Aloe Vera
- New Age Music
- Guacamole and Margaritas

Extras
- Low, Draped Table
- Custom Paint-Splattered Tablecloth
- Chartreuse Silk Cushions

Extravagances
- An Abundance of Delicate
  Butterfly Ornaments
- Mexican Hand-Blown Glasses
- Silver and Turquoise
  Table Accoutrements

TUTERA TIPS

- To get rid of smoke odors or other bad smells before an aromatherapy session, place a shallow bowl filled with white vinegar in the corner of a room for 48 hours. This helps absorb any unpleasant odors.

- Do not burn incense for a summer celebration like this. The musky aroma is too strong and heavy for a sunny afternoon party.

- *"Nunca permitan que una doncella corte cebolla, porque llora María Santísima."* (Do not let a virgin slice onions because the Blessed Virgin Mary will cry.)

- *"Nunca pongas los zapatos en la cabecera porque tendrás malas pesadillas."* (Never put your shoes at the head of the bed because you will have nightmares.)

- Purchase an inexpensive *chimanea* (an outdoor terra-cotta oven). They are terrific for outdoor entertaining, and guests love to huddle around them.

- Do not make guacamole ahead of time; the color will go off even with a lot of lemon juice. Chopping the other ingredients (onions, tomatoes, etc.) in advance can save you some time, however.

- Aloe vera is not just for sunburn. If you burn your finger, run the burn under tap water for a few minutes, pat dry, and apply fresh aloe to the burn area.

- When making frozen margaritas use crushed ice or ice chips. Large ice cubes from a tray or ice box are too big and can ruin your blender.

- When buying art, only buy pieces that truly move you. If you go with your gut feelings, you will find that you appreciate your choices more and more each day.

- When your party is over, draw a warm bath, add all your favorite aromatherapy oils, and listen to some relaxing music, as if you were re-inventing your own private Ten Thousand Waves in the mountains of Santa Fe.

Waving Goodbye to Santa Fe

I have a weakness for Santa Fe. Call me nostalgic, New Age, or sentimental, but I've never rushed to the airport after planning an event there; it's more like a reluctant trudge. What can I tell you? The ancient quality of light falling on those magical vistas of rust-colored earth is addictive. The chance to indulge in the quiet pleasure of an early morning hike through desert mountains makes that layover in the Salt Lake airport the next day seem justified. But the day after Iola's party, as I looked forward to one more day filled with the rich rewards of Santa Fe's natural offerings, I was rewarded for staying in a completely unexpected way—I ran into Iola.

When I saw her the day before, Iola had been positively aglow with radiant creativity, and everything she said and did was marked by it. But the day after the party, she seemed otherworldly. She wasn't sure if it is was the long, bright evening, the passionate conversations she'd had with old friends of hers from Paris, or the scent of lavender and almonds filling the air, but something had sifted into her consciousness. The clarity and elation she felt all night peaked when she felt her baby girl kick inside of her for the first time (practicing downward dog, perhaps?). It was then that she decided to name her baby Aurora, in honor of their earliest moment together on the summer solstice.

Now, I like to think of myself as a fairly modest guy; I can't take credit for Iola's epiphany. But in helping to create the sensual environment that inspired her so much, I felt like I had experienced something spiritual myself. In moments like that, when the planets align and everything falls into place, a party can be a magical thing, and that is the deepest imaginable reward for what I do. And so, as I watched the planes come and go through the windows of the Salt Lake airport the next day, I felt nothing but blessed.

June in Santa Fe
MENU

Courtesy of Mark Kiffin,
chef at The Compound.

Brie Soup
with Toasted Almonds

Slow-Baked Salmon
with Chardonnay-Butter Sauce

Roasted Rhubarb and
Strawberry Rustica

Brie Soup
with Toasted Almonds
(Serves 6)

1½ quarts vegetable stock, preferably homemade
1½ cups heavy cream
1½ pounds French Brie, rind removed,
 cut into 1-inch cubes
1½ shallots, peeled and finely minced
Salt and freshly ground pepper to taste
⅓ cup sliced almonds, toasted in a heavy
 skillet for 3 to 5 minutes

Put the stock and cream in a large, heavy-bottom pot and bring to a simmer over medium-low heat; be careful not to boil the cream. Add the Brie and shallots and continue to cook, stirring frequently with a wooden spoon, until the Brie softens and melts, 5 to 7 minutes. Season the soup with salt and pepper to taste.

In a blender, puree the soup in small batches until smooth and creamy. Return the soup to the pot and reheat. Ladle the soup into warmed individual serving bowls, top with the toasted almonds, and serve immediately.

Slow-Baked Salmon
with Chardonnay–Butter Sauce
(Serves 6)

3 pounds salmon fillets, skin on, pin bones removed,
*   cut into six 8-ounce portions*
Salt and freshly ground pepper to taste
3 medium carrots, peeled and sliced
1 celery root (about ¾ pound), peeled, cut into
*   ¼-inch cubes*
1½ bulbs fennel, greenery removed, cut into
*   ¼-inch cubes*
3 medium white onions, cut into ¼-inch cubes
1 large bunch fresh lovage (optional)
1 large bunch fresh thyme
1 large bunch fresh Italian parsley
1 bunch fresh basil

FOR THE SAUCE
1 cup Chardonnay
1 tablespoon champagne vinegar
1 tablespoon minced shallots
Small sprig fresh thyme
Salt and freshly ground pepper to taste
1 cup (2 sticks) unsalted butter, cut into
*   cubes and chilled*

Preheat the oven to 275° F. Season the salmon with salt and pepper and set aside.

Combine the carrots, celery root, fennel, and onions in a baking dish large enough to hold all the salmon fillets in one layer, then place the fillets on top. (Do not allow the fillets to touch the sides of the dish.)

Lay the fresh herbs on top, covering as much of the fish as possible. Cover the dish with aluminum foil and bake until the salmon is opaque in the center, about 45 minutes, or less if you prefer your salmon cooked medium or medium-rare.

Meanwhile, make the sauce: In a saucepan over medium heat, simmer the wine, vinegar, shallot, thyme, a pinch of salt, and a few turns of pepper until the liquid is reduced and slightly thickened, 5 to 7 minutes. Lower the heat and slowly stir in the butter, piece by piece. Strain through a fine-mesh sieve, taste for salt and pepper, and keep warm.

When the salmon is done, discard the herbs. Place a mound of the cooked vegetables on each of 6 warmed dinner plates, arrange a piece of salmon on top, and drizzle with the sauce.

Roasted Rhubarb and Strawberry Rustica

(Serves 6 or more)

FOR THE PASTRY DOUGH
2 cups all-purpose flour
⅓ cup sugar
Pinch salt
⅓ pound unsalted butter, cut into cubes and chilled
3 tablespoons heavy cream
1 large egg
½ teaspoon vanilla extract

FOR THE FILLING
1 pint fresh strawberries, hulled and sliced
1 stalk rhubarb, thinly sliced
2 tablespoons sugar
½ teaspoon cornstarch
Grated zest of 1 small orange

FOR THE GLAZE
1 large egg white mixed with 1 teaspoon sugar

Preheat the oven to 375° F.

Make the pastry dough: Use an electric mixer with a paddle attachment to combine the flour, sugar, and salt with the butter, mixing until crumbly, 2 to 3 minutes.

In another mixing bowl, whisk together the cream, egg, and vanilla and stir until thoroughly combined. With the mixer on low, slowly pour the cream mixture into the crumbly mixture and mix just until the dough comes together. Cover with plastic wrap, flatten the dough into a dish, and refrigerate for 1 hour.

Make the filling: Toss the strawberries, rhubarb, sugar, cornstarch, and orange zest together until the strawberries and rhubarb are evenly coated.

Roll the dough into a large circle, 10 to 12 inches across. Line a baking sheet with parchment paper, transfer the dough to the paper, and pile the filling in the center of the circle. Turn the edges in to form a rim and brush the rim with the egg white mixture. Bake for 20 minutes, or until the pastry is golden brown. Slice like a pie and serve.

July in Washington, D.C.

a patriotic poolside party
and *a sultry summer dinner*

How great is Washington, D.C.? It's a city where entertaining is considered a national imperative. Can we honestly be sure that the New Frontier would have taken off if Senator John Kennedy and Jackie Bouvier hadn't thrown all those fabulous parties? And when someone mentions Reaganomics, you have to admit that for a moment an image of Nancy Reagan lighting the official White House Christmas tree in her red cashmere Bill Blass togs crosses your mind. Washington, D.C., parties are about power and pageantry; finding that perfect balance between stately protocol and jaw-dropping glamour, discreet handshakes and enormous cocktail rings. Party politics takes on a whole new meaning as senators, reporters, and lobbyists loosen their ties and debate the hot issues while snatching canapés from silver platters and deviled eggs from the side-board, and sending the nearest Senate page to fix them a double Glenfiddich neat. And though the dinner parties are inevitably hosted in well-appointed dining rooms acces-sorized with luxe centerpieces and formal silk napkins, the sleeves are rolled up and the elbows are on the table. All in all, a good party here has a purpose.

Of course, when the heat of July sets in on the capital city the parties really heat up, too. The deep green foliage is ridiculously abundant, French doors swing open, and seersucker suits get their first pressing of the year. The season of outdoor entertaining has arrived, resplendent in dogwood blooms and illuminated by dancing fireflies and glowing hurricane lamps. I must tip my hat to the great world of Washington summer parties. Somehow even the pool parties here never devolve into straight-up sunblock and 7-Up affairs. Instead, they embody the manicured elegance typical of the city: From the white canvas umbrellas to the edged lawns to the trimmed hedges and piles of fluffy towels fresh from the dryer, great D.C. parties match the best of conservative traditions with a liberal dose of spontaneity.

Last July I was hired for a number of parties in the D.C. area. Most were extravagant and formal, decked with rare orchids and crystal chandeliers, so it was refreshing to find myself blowing up beach balls and icing cupcakes for a splashy Fourth of July backyard bash. Having grown up in a small town myself, I'm a sucker for neighborhood parties. And in D.C., when your neighbor may be the majority whip, you're bound to take the backyard seriously! But still, it wouldn't have felt like a true D.C. summer for me without an elegant patio dinner soiree on one of those long, idyllic summer nights. Jackie O. would have been proud!

Patriotic Open House Party

Everybody loves the Fourth of July, but in D.C., where the flags are already raised, the celebration of this holiday is intensified. Where else can you get Independence Day decorations as spectacular as the Washington Monument and a fireworks backdrop as meaningful as the dome of the Capitol building? Whether you're paddle boating in the Potomac, go-go dancing on a Georgetown rooftop, or wiping down the grill in your Chevy Chase garden, you'll feel the Independence Day spirit radiating from the heart of the city.

When Kaitlyn and Marcus called me to plan a Fourth of July party in their Cleveland Park backyard, I couldn't turn down an opportunity so rife with patriotic symbolism. And how glad am I that I made the effort. This couple is so D.C.: She works for the Feds, he works for the District. But the point is they work . . . and work. Even on Sunday mornings, the political talk shows are blaring on the kitchen TV set as they debate the contents of the Op-Ed page. But none of this ambition and dedication was going to get in the way of their Fourth of July party. Their die-hard commitment to community is the reason they got into politics in the first place, and it's also the reason they could not let this patriotic holiday go by without including the whole block in their festivities. This meant lots of kids, and a constant flow of guests throughout the afternoon.

When I am planning an open house party I try to create a flexible, trouble-free environment that can withstand what amounts to a series of parties within one. Durable red, white, and blue plastic beach balls by nature can never be "messed up." Whether they're filling the pool or scattered across the lawn, they always add a cheerful touch to the party. The same can be said for flag-patterned towels and blue-and-white-striped napkins. Crumpled or folded, the color scheme is unharmed. Add white wine sangria for the grown-ups, virgin sangria for the kids (made with grape juice and chunks of fruit), and the ultimate movable feast—the cupcake—and you've got more than a bunch of people getting together, you've got a community!

Open House How-to

It sounds easy and laid back, but a great open house pool party can be stressful if you're not prepared. I like to prepare almost everything in advance, from the food to the drinks to the towels by the pool. It's important that guests feel comfortable helping themselves and never have to ask for something like a towel, sunscreen, or a glass of water. The basics should be in abundance and easy to find. At Kaitlyn and Marcus's pool party, I set a playful tone by providing each arriving guest with a little gift tote packed with festive sunglasses, Silly String, lip balm, sunscreen, and a small stick of roll-on bug repellant. We also rolled up some colorful sarongs for the ladies and passed them out by the pool. These gifts indicate to the guest that they are going to be taken care of but they can also help themselves to what they need, when they need it! Here are a few alternate patriotic pool party presentation concepts:

- Position coolers or large galvanized buckets filled with small bottles of flat and sparkling water, so that your guests are always within reach of hydration.
- Line one very large white basket with a blue cloth and fill it with all your outdoor necessities from bug spray to sunblock. You can even add some Band-Aids and a bee-sting kit.
- If you don't have a lot of shade by your pool, bring out a basket of old summer hats—from fishing hats to baseball hats to fancy, wide-brimmed lady's hats—for your guests to borrow.
- Have citronella candles and umbrellas at the ready to protect your party from the evening attack of mosquitoes or the late-afternoon rainfall!
- Music is a must for any party, so if you don't have outside speakers bring out a CD player with speakers. There must always be music playing.

Follow the Bouncing Ball

A pool filled with beach balls? What's not to love? They're inexpensive, make a strong, colorful statement and add a kind of slapstick edge to your pool party. I recommend investing in an inexpensive air pump to save yourself a long morning of light-headedness and aggravation. Yes, you can substitute balloons to achieve a similar look, but remember, no helium—regular good old-fashioned air will do. As far as picking your colors, I always find that one color scheme in abundance makes for a more unified statement. For a backyard wedding, you could fill a pool with white and/or clear beach balls. For a silver anniversary, you could use silver ones. As for the Fourth, if red, white, and blue beach balls are for sale in your neck of the woods, just grab a dozen of each color.

A Can of Flowers

As a great connoisseur of all-American imagery, Andy Warhol was quick to take the Campbell's soup can and put it on the walls of a gallery. And we can follow his lead. The great thing is, the cans are still—what? sixty-nine cents a pop? I use them to hold a casual bunch of green leaves, grasses, and herbs in water. You too can make them into artful objects right in your own backyard.

- Thoroughly clean the inside of the can, without getting too much water on the outside label (to prevent wrinkling).
- With a hammer and nail, create two small holes on opposite sides of the can.
- Thread string or wire through the holes.
- Attach to the supports of an opened garden umbrella.

You can also pot small flowers or herbs in soup cans. The labels are adorable and make for a great conversation piece. You can also cover soup cans with cinnamon sticks, fresh asparagus, lemon grass, or carrots in a vertical pattern around the can. Simply coat the outside of an aluminum can with glue and tie with a piece of raffia and you've got a small organic vase to nestle between serving trays on a buffet table.

Lawn Games

When your guests start to pickle and pucker after hours of lounging in the pool, they'll be relieved when you tell them about all the great lawn activities you've prepared! For long summer parties, activities are a blessing. Even naysayers and wallflowers will be thanking you after a hilarious, if intensely competitive, game of horseshoes or croquet! Here are my favorites:

Frisbee	Especially if there is a dog to occupy! This will keep Fido from licking your neighbors' faces all afternoon.
Boules	Great for the Francophiles in your life and easy to learn (though hard to play!)
Horseshoes	Old-fashioned? Yes. Boring? No. This game looks so pretty on the lawn, and it's pleasantly addictive.
Volleyball	Okay, you will need a net, a good deal of space, and an eager player who'll run and fetch the ball when it flies over the fence into Mr. McTrundle's yard!
Twister	What can I say? You'll have funny tan lines if you play this game outside in the sun.
Croquet	Proper and posh, this game will get the golfers out of their banana loungers!

Ready and Waiting: A Simple Red, White, and Blue Menu

For an all-day party you want fresh, yummy ingredients, simple and easy serving techniques, and fuss-free preparation. In other words, you want to be able to pull a beautifully arranged dish from the fridge, yank off the saran wrap, and serve to awestruck guests. Make sure you are careful to replenish the food throughout the afternoon. You do not want your stunning chilled buffet to become a sea of wilted lettuce and beading cheese. In addition to the freshness factor, you never want your late-arriving guests to feel as if you have run out of food and drink: It should always appear as if the party has just begun. Here's what we served at the Washingtons' party to raves and repeat visits to the buffet bar . . .

- A big bowl of red cherries
- Greek salad with feta, cherry tomatoes, and olives
- Toasted bagel chips and whitefish spread
- Strawberries with crème fraîche
- Loaves of french baguettes
- Crisp apple slices
- Slices of smoked ham off the bone with honey mustard sauce
- Chilled crab cakes
- Cold fried chicken (can be made the day before)

Quenching the Thirst

Sangria is a very clever drink for an afternoon party on a hot day because it has all the refreshing qualities of an iced cocktail with the alcohol content of wine. Okay, maybe the brandy takes it up a notch, but the fruit juice does cut its potency. To make the best sangria, allow the fruit to soak overnight. For an all-day open-house party, I recommend making twice this much for every four guests.

My Favorite Sangria

(Serves 6 to 8)

One 1.5-liter bottle red wine,
   preferably Cabernet Sauvignon
1 cup sugar, plus more to taste
3 ounces brandy, plus more to taste
1 large lemon, sliced
1 large orange, sliced
1 large apple, cored and cut into very thin slices
About 2¼ cups chilled seltzer water,
   preferably orange or lemon flavored

1. Mix all the ingredients except the seltzer in a large nonreactive container, stir, and let sit in the refrigerator for 18 to 24 hours. The most delightful sangria is produced when the fruit is allowed to soak in the wine at least overnight.
2. When you are ready to serve, stir the wine mixture, then add more sugar or brandy to taste. The sangria should be fairly strong and rather sweet—almost syrupy.
3. For each serving, pour ¾ cup of the wine mixture into a wineglass and stir in ¼ cup of the seltzer. Drink and enjoy.

Summer Sangria

1 orange
1 lemon
One 750-milliliter bottle dry white wine
2 tablespoons sugar
1 ounce brandy
1 ounce Cointreau
2 cups ice cubes
1 cup club soda

1. Cut the orange in half and cut one half into thin slices; juice the other half and put both the slices and juice in a large nonreactive container.
2. Cut the lemon into thin slices and add to the container, along with the wine, sugar, brandy, and Cointreau. Stir to combine, then refrigerate to chill.
3. Before serving, add the ice and club soda and stir gently. Serve in highball or Collins glasses.

Three E's

Essentials
- Sangria
- Cherries, Apples, Berries
- Red, White, and Blue Tablecloth and Napkins

Extras
- Red, White, and Blue Beach Balls (at least twenty)
- Campbell's Soup Hanging Planters
- White Garden Umbrellas

Extravagances
- American Flag Towels and Blankets
- Summer Party Gifts Bags
- Authentic French Boules, or Complete Croquet Set

TUTERA TIPS

• When guests arrive, show them the best route from house to garden so as to avoid every door being opened and every floor being exposed to the odd dripping body.

• Position a few comfortable chairs and a low table next to the pool for the adults to use while they're on duty watching the kids splash in the pool.

• If entertaining outdoors at night, make sure to put wonderful luminaries around the perimeter of the pool. Not only does it look beautiful, but it adds safety too.

• Make homemade smoothie popsicles from your favorite smoothie recipes. Adults and kids love them.

An Elegant
Al Fresco Dinner

Not everybody has a stone balustrade in their backyard, and that's okay. Not everybody has neoclassical gold- and blue-trimmed china, and that's also okay. And though the First Lady has more White House place-setting possibilities than she'll ever even know, the point is, all you need is one well-dressed table to make you feel like the first lady of your own home.

Washingtonians revel in their formality and pageantry. They don't think twice about hauling all those elegant dining room accoutrements out to the patio, and you shouldn't either. Dining to the sound of crickets chirping high in the trees while crystal glasses clink across the table is one

of the rare pleasures of outdoor entertaining. It is also one of the most peaceful sounds I know, and is the quintessential local detail that I return to over and over when planning outdoor dinner parties.

Joy and Jason called me with a special request. When I planned their gorgeous winter wedding two years ago, Joy and I talked and talked about the charms of the Washington summer. At the time, we were up to our elbows in roses and velvet, but she never forgot my poetic waxing about crickets and crystal. So when the in-laws descended on Joy and Jason's Chevy Chase home for a summer visit, Joy called me to ask if I could help her capture that per-fect sound. Needless to say, she didn't exactly have to twist my arm.

Once the table was set, I recognized another unique and charming quality of the Washington table. Each place setting displays a bold confidence in color and line that commands attention. The blue and gold china is a nod to the pageantry of the West Wing; the luxuriant brocade tablecloth captures the simple charm of a Georgian parlor. A stunning variety of crystal goblets, a pair of vintage decanters, and a tiny bundle of lily of the valley elegantly fuse the formal and the floral; the crickets have ample reason to sing.

A Delightful Summer Repast

There are many chefs along the respective coasts of this great nation who claim to be able to create the superior crab cake. From southern Georgia to western Alaska, folks have debated such pressing issues as bread-crumbs versus cornmeal and soy versus Worcestershire, all the while hailing the virtues of their local crab-meat. And though it's technically the bordering state of Maryland that "is for crabs," the finest kitchens in Washington, D.C., treat the crab cake as a good French bistro treats its steak au poivre: with the utmost respect. That said, Chef Brian McBride, of Melrose Restaurant in D.C.'s fashionable West End Park Hyatt, makes a crab cake that demands not just respect, but straight-up Aretha-style R-E-S-P-E-C-T. Having worked with him many times, I have happily devoured more than one of these light, crispy, ocean-fresh delicacies, and they are consistently phenomenal. Knowing that Joy and Jason were looking to make a splash without a fuss, I knew that the famous Melrose Crab Cake, both humble and magnificent, had to be served in their glowing midsummer garden.

It was more than the crab cakes, though. McBride's overall approach to food was perfect for the Rothenbergs' elegantly relaxed dinner. Dedicated regulars at Melrose return for his simple, innovative cuisine, which takes advantage of the local seafood and blends delicate flavors and seasonings into dishes that are not only pleasing to the palate, but to the eye as well. The late light of the season allowed Joy, Jason, and their respective parents to appreciate both of these qualities. The early sweetness of McBride's Chilled Puree of Summer Peas charmed with bright accents of Lemon Verbena, Truffle-Scented Crème Fraîche, and tender pea shoots, but also with its subtle presentation. The revered crab cakes (I'll say no more of them), which arrived with a luscious dollop of Rémoulade and a medley of Grilled Summer Vegetables, graced the table with a delicious array of colors, while a vibrant Watercress Salad invigorated all the senses. By the time night fell on the garden, a Blueberry, Coconut, and Lime Crumble with Coconut Ice Cream took the edge off the warmth. And because the entire meal was so effortless to prepare, to serve, and to enjoy, the six revelers were able to savor every note of the crickets' symphony.

Topiaries:
Living Bouquets

The great thing about a topiary centerpiece is that it adds a living, blossoming aspect to your formal setting. A topiary is kind of like a bonsai tree, except you mold the leaves instead of shaping the trunk. Topiaries are also useful because they last forever, so long as you sun, water, and trim them. They are especially nice alongside glass and crystal. A topiary isn't hard to make. Think of it this way: You are merely grooming a plant into a special shape. If you make a mistake, it's like a bad haircut—initially painful to look at, but certain to grow back in time. And this brings me to an important point: While making a topiary isn't rocket science, it does take time. If you don't want to make the effort, you can purchase premade topiaries. They can be relatively inexpensive, depending on the type and size of the plant.

Color Checklist

To capture the glorious but refined tone that exemplifies Washington, D.C., Joy and I used a palette of blue and gold—the colors of Air Force One (the ultimate symbol of presidential chic). And to add a softer, more feminine touch, we infused our decorations with a Parisian flair—paying homage to D.C.'s French heritage. Just imagine that L'Enfant left behind a few French Provincial linens after he mapped out the city!

BLUE AND WHITE
Damask Floral Tablecloth, Striped Napkins, Blue-Trimmed China, Blue-Etched Crystal, Wedgwood Blue Candles.

CRYSTAL AND GOLD
Ornate Crystal Champagne Bucket, Tiffany Crystal Candlesticks, Gold Salt and Pepper Shakers, Gold Flatware.

- Each blue-and-white napkin was tied with a handmade ribbon napkin ring.

- In the center of the table, an ornate crystal champagne bucket held a manicured ivy topiary. The base of the champagne bucket had three small white porcelain containers, each displaying a nosegay of lily of the valley.

- Each place setting used the wide blue band presidential state china, with crystal water jugs and champagne flutes and blue-etched crystal wineglasses.

- A crystal wine decanter filled with white wine was set off nicely by beautiful gold salt and pepper shakers.

Tough Flowers for Tough Heat

Although Joy and I decided that due to the lush surroundings and humid weather, we'd forgo lots of bouquets of cut flowers, we wanted a living centerpiece for this elegant garden party. The subtle and exquisite smelling lily of the valley blossoms were displayed in potted soil rather than snipped. If you're planning a more floral look to your July table, you should know which flowers withstand heat and humidity with grace. Here is the winner of my tough summer flower contest: Roses! For decorating your table during the sweltering heat of a Washington summer, roses are an excellent choice. Maybe that's why there's a rose garden at the White House. You can also try orchids, pincushion protea, delphinium, and blossoms from the aster family such as monte casino, florentines, and crown aster.

The Perfect Mint Julep

Washington may be a political powerhouse, but it's also got all the charm of a small Southern town, not to mention the sweltering summers! Mint Juleps are perhaps the most refreshing of the dark liquor drinks, with the possible exception of a Whisky Sour. They are a real conversation starter too: Folks have debated the way to make a proper mint julep since the first bottle of bourbon was uncorked. I find that the best juleps are those that have a little time to steep.

6 sprigs fresh mint
1 teaspoon superfine sugar
3 ounces bourbon

1. With a muddler, mash the mint and the sugar in the bottom of a Collins glass.
2. Fill the glass with crushed ice and add the bourbon. Stir the mixture vigorously with a bar spoon.
3. Let steep for about 5 minutes, then enjoy!

Three E's

Essentials
- Blue-and-White China
- Tapered Candles
- Crab Cakes

Extras
- Lily of the Valley
- Blue-and-White Damask Table Linens
- Ivy Topiaries

Extravagances
- Crystal Glasses and Decanter
- Crystal Tiffany Candlesticks
- Crystal Champagne Bucket

TUTERA TIPS

• Reuse small glass or pottery candle containers as miniature vases for flower arrangements.

• When entertaining outdoors during the summer months, always make sure to have plenty of chilled water available for your guests.

• For summer entertaining, a chilled soup first course is one of my favorites. It's a light and refreshing way to get started.

• If you are just starting to buy crystal stemware, begin by purchasing one type of glass. This way you can mix them with basic stemware and still have a great look until you complete the set.

• When entertaining, seat couples on separate sides of the table to create more opportunity for lively and integrated conversation.

Traditions, Tried and True

I don't know if Joy and Jason's parents noticed the crickets and the crystal, the subtle hint of truffle oil in the crème fraîche, or the faint perfume of lily of the valley flowers drifting up from the centerpiece, but I do know that they stayed up talking and laughing well into the night. Like kids, they filled a wine bottle with fireflies. Like teens, they devoured seconds of every course. Like adults, they managed to discuss just enough front-page news before turning their attention to more serious matters: a riotous reminiscence of Joy and Jason's wedding reception. Joy called me the next day to inform me that Jason's mother refused to leave town without the crab cake recipe! She also asked if I were free for a repeat performance next summer. I felt so honored to have become a part of a new tradition for these two families. It's the joy of knowing that special memories are being created each time I help bring people together that makes it all worthwhile.

As I headed off to Dulles airport, I thought about Joy and Jason. How inspiring it was to see the two families establish an annual tradition of meeting for one long, laughter-filled dinner party. They give dinner with the in-laws a good name. I also thought about Kaitlyn and Marcus. How inspiring it was to witness their passion for public service translate into a wonderful pool party for the whole neighborhood. This town may be known for its stately charm, coiffed topiaries, and historic buildings but it's the energetic character of its citizens, and the parties they love to host, that keep me coming back!

July in Washington, D.C.
MENU

Courtesy of Brian McBride,
chef of Melrose at the Park Hyatt Hotel.

Chilled Puree of Summer Peas

with Lemon Verbena and Truffle-Scented
Crème Fraîche

Jumbo Lump Crab Cakes

with Rémoulade, Grilled Summer Vegetables,
and Watercress Salad

Blueberry, Coconut,
and Lime Crumble

with Coconut Ice Cream

Chilled Puree of Summer Peas

with Lemon Verbena and Truffle-Scented
Crème Fraîche
(Serves 6)

2 tablespoons unsalted butter
1 large onion, diced
2 ribs celery, diced
Salt and freshly ground pepper to taste
4 cups chicken stock, preferably homemade
4 pounds fresh green peas, shelled (to yield 2 pounds)
4 sprigs fresh thyme
½ cup heavy cream
1 bunch lemon verbena, leaves only; or
*   1 inch lemon grass, tough outer layers removed,*
*   coarsely chopped (to yield 2 tablespoons)*

FOR THE CRÈME FRAÎCHE
½ cup crème fraîche, chilled
3 teaspoons white truffle oil

TO SERVE (OPTIONAL)
1 large bunch pea shoots (see Note)
Good-quality fruity olive oil

Put the butter in a large pot and melt it over low heat. Add the onion and celery, season with salt and pepper, and cook over low to medium heat until the onion is translucent but still firm, 5 to 7 minutes. Meanwhile, bring the stock to a boil in another pot.

Add the peas to the onion-celery mixture and stir to combine. Add the hot stock and the thyme and bring to a boil over medium-high heat. Reduce the heat to low, stir in the heavy cream, and simmer for 3 to 5 minutes.

Transfer the soup to a blender, add the lemon verbena, and puree. Strain the puree through a fine-mesh sieve or chinois and immediately pour it into a bowl set in a larger bowl of ice water; chill, stirring occasionally, for 5 to 7 minutes. Speedy cooling is key to giving this soup its appealing green color. Put soup plates in the refrigerator to chill.

Put the crème fraîche and the truffle oil in a bowl and season with salt and pepper. Whisk until the crème fraîche becomes slightly stiff, 3 to 5 minutes.

Ladle the soup into the chilled soup plates. Spoon a dollop of the crème fraîche mixture on top of each serving and sprinkle with the pea shoots, if using. Drizzle with the oil, if desired.

NOTE: Fresh pea shoots are the leaves and shoots of a young pea plant. They are tender and sweet, and their strong pea flavor is a delicious addition to this soup.

Jumbo Lump Crab Cakes

with Rémoulade, Grilled Summer Vegetables,
and Watercress Salad

(Serves 6 or more)

3 pounds jumbo lump crabmeat
2 tablespoons Dijon mustard
3 large eggs
¼ cup chopped fresh Italian parsley
3 drops Tabasco Sauce
1 teaspoon Worcestershire sauce
Salt and freshly ground pepper to taste
¾ cup fresh white breadcrumbs
¼ cup clarified butter or extra-virgin olive oil
1 recipe Grilled Summer Vegetables (page 132)
1 recipe Watercress Salad (page 132)
1 recipe Rémoulade (page 132)

Pick over the crabmeat for shells and discard them, being careful not to break up the lumps of crabmeat. Put in a mixing bowl and set aside.

In another mixing bowl, combine the mustard, eggs, parsley, Tabasco, and Worcestershire, whisk together, and season with salt and pepper.

Pour the egg mixture over the crabmeat and gently combine with your hands, taking care not to break up the chunks of crabmeat. Gently fold in the breadcrumbs. The crab cake mixture should be loose and wet, not dry. Mold the mixture into sixteen 3½-ounce crab cakes and refrigerate until serving time.

When you're almost ready to serve, preheat the oven to 400°. Divide the clarified butter between two sauté pans and heat it over medium heat. When the butter is hot, add the crab cakes and cook for about 2 minutes on each side, until browned. Place on a baking sheet and transfer to the oven until cooked through, about 10 minutes.

Arrange the grilled vegetables and the salad on warm dinner plates and place 2 or 3 crab cakes on each plate. Serve the Rémoulade on the side.

Rémoulade
(Makes about 2½ cups)

2 cups prepared mayonnaise
2 anchovy fillets, fresh or canned
(rinse to remove excess salt), chopped (optional)
¼ cup chopped fresh Italian parsley
⅓ cup cornichons
Juice of ½ lemon (about 1½ tablespoons)
1 tablespoon drained capers
2 drops Tabasco Sauce
1 teaspoon Worcestershire sauce
1 clove garlic, minced

Combine all the ingredients in a medium bowl and whisk together. Refrigerate until needed; the Rémoulade will keep for 1 week or more if refrigerated in an airtight container.

Grilled Summer Vegetables
(Serves 6)

4 large zucchini, trimmed and sliced
¼ inch thick
6 tomatoes, trimmed and sliced ¼ inch thick
4 red bell peppers, seeded and sliced ¼ inch thick
2 pounds asparagus (about 40 stalks)
½ cup extra-virgin olive oil
Salt and freshly ground pepper to taste
1 teaspoon chopped fresh rosemary leaves

Prepare a charcoal fire or preheat a gas or stovetop grill to medium-high.
   Toss the vegetables with the oil, salt and pepper, and rosemary, then spread them on the grill. Grill until al dente, 2 to 3 minutes per side. Remove from the grill and serve warm.

Watercress Salad
(Serves 6)

2 bunches very fresh watercress
2 tablespoons lemon mosto olive oil (or 1½ tablespoons
olive oil mixed with 1 teaspoon fresh lemon juice)
Salt and freshly ground pepper to taste

Wash the watercress and trim off the very bottom of the stems. Transfer to a nonreactive bowl and toss with the oil and salt and pepper.

Blueberry, Coconut, and Lime Crumble *with Coconut Ice Cream*

(Serves 6 or more)

FOR THE LIME CURD
1 cup fresh lime juice (from about 10 limes)
¾ cup (1½ sticks) unsalted butter
4 large eggs
¾ cup sugar
Grated zest of 2 limes (about 2 teaspoons)

FOR THE TOPPING
1 cup all-purpose flour
¼ cup brown sugar
⅓ cup granulated sugar
6 tablespoons (¾ stick) unsalted butter
1 cup shredded unsweetened coconut
2 pints fresh blueberries

TO SERVE
Confectioners' sugar
1 recipe Coconut Ice Cream (recipe follows)

Make the lime curd: Heat the lime juice and butter in a saucepan over medium-high heat until the mixture comes to a boil. In a mixing bowl, whisk the eggs together with the sugar.

Slowly pour the boiling lime juice mixture into the egg mixture, stirring constantly to combine. Return the mixture to the saucepan and cook over medium heat until it becomes thick and starts to boil again, 3 to 5 minutes. Stir in the lime zest and refrigerate for at least 1 hour.

Make the topping: Mix the flour, brown sugar, granulated sugar, and butter in a mixing bowl using a wooden spoon until the mixture becomes crumbly, forming lumps about the size of a peanut. Stir in the coconut.

Preheat the oven to 375° F.

Spread the lime curd in a 10-inch pie pan. Top with the blueberries. Evenly spread the crumble topping over the berries and bake until the topping is brown and bubbly at the edges, 30 to 40 minutes.

Dust each serving of the crumble with confectioners' sugar, and top with a scoop of ice cream. Serve warm.

Coconut Ice Cream

(Serves 6 or more)

1 can (15 ounces) sweetened cream of coconut (I like Coco Lopez)
2 cups milk
1 cup heavy cream
1 teaspoon vanilla extract
½ teaspoon coconut extract
Pinch salt

Mix together all the ingredients and process in an ice cream machine. Freeze for at least 6 hours before serving.

August in Nantucket

send–off–the–summer soiree on the beach

When posh New Englanders seek refuge from the dog days of August, they're often found on Nantucket—that famed island where summer parties are treated as a high art. Though china, linens, and silver might be on hand, the cause for celebration is always simple: a sunset, the passing of the tall-masted boats, or a send-off for friends returning to the mainland.

Very few people have been to Nantucket only once. For those who are lucky enough to wander through the low brush to a friend's quaint shingled cottage, savor a crisp, ice-cold glass of pinot grigio on the beach at dusk, or watch the sun crack over the eastern horizon of America, this small island becomes not just a destination, but a way of life, and perhaps even a religion. The families who return year after year have perfected the kind of casual opulence that serves as the single antidote to the thick, heavy heat of late summer. Entertaining becomes the cultural equivalent of a sea breeze sweeping off Nantucket Sound: The food is fresh and simple, less about measuring cups and recipes than about stopping for a pint of those plump, freshly picked raspberries on the way home from the beach, or steaming lobsters with the right group of friends.

For our hosts, Meghan and Brian, the "right" group is made up of eight people who are near to their hearts, but unfortunately, not to their Boston townhouse. Each August, they swallow their pride and have an honest-to-God *Big Chill*–style reunion. For one week of the year, they forget about the breaking stories they cover for *The Boston Globe,* and enjoy the comfort of old friends who can still rib Meghan about her stint as a Beat poet, and Brian about his extensive collection of heavy metal T-shirts. Since this close-knit circle gets together so rarely, every night is a "last night"; it's a standing joke among them. If it's not the "last first night together," it's the "last night before we return our rented bikes."

Whatever the occasion, there's always a cause for celebration. For their real "last night together," Meghan and Brian asked me to help them throw the ultimate "last night" party, an affair that could pay sufficient tribute to the week they spent lounging around telling stories to each other and fighting over their only September issue of *Vanity Fair*, but also to the splendor of summer in Nantucket. I could tell by their bare feet and easy camaraderie that fussy and formal were completely out of the question. Nevertheless, this party had to measure up: to their friendship, to their obvious joie de vivre, and to the riches of summer.

By five o'clock on the evening of the party, I was already on the propeller plane heading back to New York, content with the knowledge that everything would go exactly as planned. Usually I stay at a party until the last tablecloth has been bundled up for laundering, but on this occasion, the challenge was to prepare every inch of the party beforehand so that the hosts and their guests could unpack this party like a picnic—but of course, one worthy of the great Gatsby himself. I wanted the guests to feel as if they'd stumbled upon a private dining room on a deserted beach, where they would open four coolers to find a delicious summer dinner just waiting to be enjoyed. A far cry from their days of Iron Maiden T-shirts and black berets, but then again, on every "last night" something new begins.

A Four-Star Picnic Using Fresh Local Ingredients

This may have been a beach party, but I saw no reason to skimp on the good stuff. During cocktails, I served salmon caviar in a shimmery mother-of-pearl bowl set atop a matching seashell-shaped bowl filled with ice. The meal I designed with master New England chef Donald Kolp did await Meghan and her Big Chill posse on the beach, but there were no wax paper–wrapped sandwiches or apple juice snack packs in sight. Just as this group graduated from college-styled pizza parties to Brie and baguette wine parties, this meal showed real progress. And progression was toward local, Nantucket ingredients: big, fresh oysters and that morning's catch of Atlantic yellowfin tuna.

The meal was a triumph of seafood simplicity, the kind of meal you can serve on a well-appointed dining table (such as those at the Brant Point Grill, where Donald is executive chef) or on the beach beneath the amber glow of a late summer sunset. One of the characteristics of Donald's award-winning cuisine is his knack for combining the simplest fresh seafood preparation with playful, innovative sauces. Here, he brings cranberries into the mix, a nod to the local crop and a taste of the autumn to come. They appear in the sweet roasted orange and cranberry vinaigrette that he uses to spice up a crisp Bartlett Farm's Field Greens Salad topped with Grilled Nantucket Oysters; and again in a savory Cranberry Steak Sauce for his Mesquite-Grilled Yellowfin Tuna with Grilled New Potatoes. Cranberry Bread Pudding with Bourbon Caramel Sauce and Spiced Pecans are a fitting finale to this four-star picnic.

Beach Party

As much as we dream of the sand, sun, and surf all winter long, these elements pose their own challenges when it comes to seaside entertaining. Without dwelling on the sensation of biting into a sandy apple, let's just say that a few tricks of the trade can keep your beach party from becoming unnecessarily sticky and sandy. The overarching principle here is to adapt. When on the beach, act like you're on the beach. Just as your favorite summer heels will get you nowhere in the sand, trying to light your candelabra in the sea breeze is a serious exercise in futility. Be prepared for the elements, and then you will be left alone to enjoy them. Here's how.

Outdoor Rooms:
Bringing It All Outside

When entertaining outdoors, I find that a few simple arrangements can transform an open space into a structured space. The canopy walls of my beach party not only define the party area, they evoke the large, white ship sails flapping in the wind off Nantucket Sound. When used to separate the central dining area from smaller groupings of chairs around its perimeter, they also allow guests to move freely between a series of small outdoor rooms.

- Dig five 2-foot-deep holes about 8 feet apart in the sand.
- Insert five 8- to 10-foot wooden poles into the holes and firmly pack sand around the openings, until the poles are steadied and standing upright.
- Tie a very strong cord or rope about 6 inches below the tops of the poles.
- Attach sheer white, cream, or beige curtains to 8-foot wooden curtain rods.
- Attach the curtain rods to the poles where the cord or rope is attached.

Musical Chairs

A mix of different chairs adds eclectic charm to a casual party. At Meghan and Brian's beach party, I assembled a long bench, a few armchairs, and the odd wooden chair. Guests could lounge on the bigger chairs while having a cocktail and then move up to the wooden bench to snack on berries and enjoy a candlelit dinner. As the sun set and the stars came out, guests could curl up in the large blankets strewn over some of the chairs.

Packed and Ready to Go: Portable Party

Those big green Coleman coolers aren't just for camping anymore; they're the ultimate transport for your movable feast. No matter where you are, if you're partying al fresco, these efficient cold cases seriously cut down on the number of times the screen door slams shut. But to prevent guests from fishing for beers in sludgy ice, pack your coolers as a dapper gentleman might his Hermès valise.

• Arrange your food, garnishes and all, before packing your coolers. The wind and the sand on the beach could lead to a gritty situation.

• You don't want your grilled yellowfin crushing your raspberry and rhubarb pies, so use four wineglasses and a cookie sheet to create a "shelf" in your cooler.

• Separate courses in separate coolers! And drinks get a cooler all to themselves.

• Never use loose ice in a cooler full of food. Seal your ice in Ziploc bags, or purchase reusable, plastic "ice" blocks.

• Old-fashioned white gauze or netting makes an elegant alternative to cling wrap and foil, and also helps fend off flying insects looking for a free meal.

Beach Etiquette

Okay, so it's almost a contradiction in terms. The beach is a place to kick off your shoes and let the cuffs of your chinos get wet with the fizz and foam of shallow breaking waves. But any seasoned beach lover knows that some things belong on the beach—not in your shoes, not in your drink, not in your food—and sand is one of them. Here are my methods for keeping order: Use a rattan basket to hold your guests' shoes while they mingle on the beach. If a hose is available, place stacks of beige- and cream-colored towels in rattan baskets next to it. Don't forget to provide an empty basket for the used towels! And finally, grab a straw or antique hand broom before you run down to the beach. This can be used to brush off chairs and the tabletop.

She Sells Seashells. . .

Who needs to go into town for flowers when there are plenty of seashells underfoot? I love working with the available elements to create table décor, from the centerpiece to the lighting. As soon as guests sit down they are greeted with a vision of pretty white seashells in abundance: open clamshells display their names, miniature shells are pressed onto the surface of decorative spheres, and shell-covered rings hold damask and silk napkins. In amongst all of this they will discover a sparkle of small crystals, and pearls that I scattered across the table to leave a reminder of sea salt and oysters. Got shells? Here's how to use 'em!

- Make shell-covered napkin rings by cutting a cardboard cylinder (from a finished roll of paper towels) into one-inch sections. Cover or spray with glue. Roll the cylinder in crushed seashells and let sit to dry.
- Glue shells around the base of a pillar candle to create a customized look.
- Glue shells around the edge of a small wall mirror to create a seaside shell frame.
- Add loose shells to a glass bowl of your favorite summer potpourri to add a subtle hint of the beach to your aromatherapy.

Place Card Holders and Pearly Plates

If you decide to get fancy for your beach dinner party, or if it is a larger party such as a wedding, why not prop up place cards in little seashells? This is a lovely way to make a formal gesture with a found object! To complement the seashell décor try serving with pearl-colored bowls and serving dishes. They add just the right luster and character to a seafood or seaside dinner. One way to bring out the shimmer of these pretty pearl bowls is to place them on soft, brown leather charger plates and surround them with sleek silverware. Here's how to fashion a seashell place card.

- Use a paint pen to write each guest's name on a small ivory card.
- Prop the label into the open "jaw" of a cleaned and dried oyster shell and tilt it to the side.

Summer White Wines

I am usually a red wine devotee, but when I'm standing on a beach at the end of a long, sunny day I find that there is nothing better than a sip of chilled white wine. Here are some of my favorites:

Banfi Fontanelle Chardonnay
Heron Chardonnay
Pepperwood Grove Sauvignon Blanc or Viognier
Louis Moreau Chablis
Louis Latour Chardonnay Grande Ardeche
Laetitia Chardonnay
Nobilo Sauvignon Blanc

Four Pretty Summer Cocktails

These are great summer cocktails for any occasion, but they are a must for beach picnics like this one. Unlike many other warm-weather concoctions, they taste just as cool and fresh when made individually as they do when premixed and stored in a pitcher. These recipes call for adding a lot of ice when serving, but not before—nobody likes a watery cocktail.

Startini

1½ ounces Belvedere vodka
1½ ounces strained fresh lemonade
¼ ounce Grand Marnier
⅛ ounce Chambord
Star fruit, sliced

1. Put the vodka, lemonade, Grand Marnier, Chambord, and plenty of ice cubes in a cocktail shaker.
2. Shake well and strain into a martini glass.
3. Garnish with a slice of star fruit.

Margarita Dream

2 ounces tequila (I recommend Patrón Silver)
2 ounces Chambord
1 ounce sour mix
1 ounce Rose's lime juice
1 ounce cranberry juice
Lime wedge

1. Put plenty of ice cubes and all the ingredients except the lime wedge in a cocktail shaker.
2. Shake well and pour into a low cocktail or margarita glass and garnish with the lime wedge.

NOTE: To create a frozen margarita, just process the ingredients in a blender.

Summer in the City

I dreamed up this delicious cocktail and presented it on ABC's *The View*.

2 ounces Belvedere vodka
2 ounces fresh lemonade
1 ounce peach nectar
½ ounce mango nectar
Edible flower, such as a pansy, or a peach slice

1. Put the vodka, lemonade, peach and mango nectars, and plenty of ice cubes in a cocktail shaker.
2. Shake well and strain into a chilled martini glass. Garnish with a single flower or a slice of peach.

Sea Breeze

2 ounces vodka, preferably Belvedere
3 ounces cranberry juice
1 ounce grapefruit juice
Lime wedge

1. Fill a highball glass with ice cubes and pour in the vodka.
2. Add the cranberry juice, then top off with the grapefruit juice. Do not stir.
3. Garnish with the lime wedge.

Three E's

Essentials
- Scattered Seashells
- Cranberries—in Every Recipe
- White Wine

Extras
- Seashell Napkin Rings
- White and Tan Table Linens
- Rattan Baskets

Extravagances
- Canopy
- Rattan Cushions and Chairs
- Caviar

TUTERA TIPS

- For a holiday island party, send a message in a bottle in lieu of an invitation. Handwrite an invitation in black ink on ivory paper, roll it into a tube, and tie with a piece of string. Funnel the scrolled invitation into an empty, clear bottle. Cork it, or screw the top back on and hand-deliver to the doorsteps of your fellow-vacationing neighbors.

- Arrange small bushels of berries in the center of your table for a colorful addition to your seaside centerpiece. Yummy for dessert too.

- Create sparkling seaside napkins by ironing what are known as "iron-on crystals" to the edges of each napkin. These iron-ons can be purchased at party and sewing supply stores.

- When entertaining outdoors, use unbreakable containers with tight lids. Tupperware makes a wonderful line of colorful containers that add charm to any beach party. They also make festive cocktail stirrers.

- Use a large conch as a candle. Find a shell that sits upright with its mouth to the sky. Drop a string wick in, and while holding it in place pour the melted wax of another candle into the shell.

- When entertaining outdoors, take along a first aid kit for that unexpected scratch or bite. Your guests will be glad you did.

- For an indoor party with an outdoor beach look, create a custom runner (made from Lucite or plastic) and fill it with sand, shells, beach grasses, and tall candles. Your guests will be hearing the ocean when they lay their eyes on this.

- If you're bringing "the beach" indoors, place a few colorful beach balls in the corners of the party space; decorate cocktail tables with glass bowls filled with dyed-blue water and floating votives.

- If you get sunburned, soak in a lukewarm bathtub filled with water and strong black tea: Add eight tea bags to boiling water, remove from heat and let steep for five minutes. Remove tea bags and pour the tea into your bath. Sit and relax for twenty minutes. The tannins in the cool black tea will soothe you.

- If you find shells on the beach and you want to use them inside, sterilize them by placing them in boiling water for at least five minutes. This helps get rid of the fishy smell.

Until We Meet Next August

The day after the party, Meghan called me to say that aside from the skipping James Taylor CD, she, her husband, and their friends had a last night to end all last nights. And with great satisfaction, I imagined them dancing on the beach at 4 AM, knowing that the innocence and energy of this late-summer fete would carry them through the next fifty-one weeks, until they could meet again. Just the thought of the cool, breezy Nantucket nights, the long, lazy days full of well-loved paperbacks, and the meandering bike rides to the lighthouses that dot the coast will return them to their time together.

Whether you throw this party on the beaches of Nantucket or poolside in San Diego, at the heart of this party is the desire to stop and take the time to savor the people and places that you love. Not to mention the taste of a late-summer, marshmallow-stuffed, graham-crunching s'more. Yes, that's right, Meghan discovered the little basket of graham crackers, Hershey bars, and marshmallows I tucked under the table. The next thing this group of old friends knew, they were all debating (with the kind of vigor only a group of cutthroat journalists could summon on such a peaceful night) the pros and cons of charbroiling versus lightly browning a marshmallow crust. These treats never fail to bring out the eight-year-old summer camper in all of us.

August in Nantucket
MENU

Courtesy of Donald Kolp,
chef at the Brant Point Grill
at the White Elephant.

Bartlett Farm's Field Greens Salad
*with Lightly Grilled Nantucket Oysters and
Roasted Orange-Cranberry Vinaigrette*

**Mesquite-Grilled
Local Yellowfin Tuna**
with Cranberry Steak Sauce and Grilled New Potatoes

Cranberry Bread Pudding
with Bourbon Caramel Sauce and Spiced Pecans

Bartlett Farm's Field Greens
Salad *with Lightly Grilled Nantucket Oysters and Roasted Orange-Cranberry Vinaigrette*
(Serves 6)

*36 fresh Nantucket oysters or
    other Atlantic oysters
1 pound mixed greens
1 recipe Roasted Orange-Cranberry
    Vinaigrette (recipe follows)*

Prepare a charcoal fire and scrub the oysters.

When the coals are hot (they will be white), place the oysters, flat side up, on the hottest part of the grill. An oyster is done when the top shell begins to open, about 1 minute. Take the oysters off the grill as they finish cooking, then remove and discard the top shells.

Put the mixed greens in a nonreactive bowl and toss lightly with the vinaigrette, taking care not to overdress the greens. Place a mound of the greens in the center of each plate and arrange the oysters around the greens. Serve immediately.

Roasted Orange-Cranberry Vinaigrette
(Makes about 3 cups)

*1 orange
½ cup unsweetened dried cranberries
½ cup cranberry juice
¼ cup orange juice
¾ cup extra-virgin olive oil
1 tablespoon cider vinegar
1 tablespoon fresh lemon juice
Salt and freshly ground pepper to taste*

Preheat the oven to 400° F.

Roast the whole orange in the oven (place a cookie sheet on the rack underneath in case it drips), turning it often until it's golden brown all over, 5 to 7 minutes. Set aside to cool completely.

Put the dried cranberries and cranberry juice in a small saucepan and bring to a boil; cook until the cranberries are soft, 8 to 10 minutes.

Cut the orange into quarters and put the entire orange, including the peel, in a blender. Pulse it several times to chop but not puree it. Add the orange juice and pulse a few more times. Strain through a fine-mesh sieve into a bowl; discard the solids. Return the juice to the blender, add the cranberry mixture, and puree until smooth.

Pour the puree into a nonreactive bowl and, using a whisk, slowly incorporate the oil. Add the vinegar and lemon juice and season with salt and pepper.

Mesquite-Grilled Local Yellowfin Tuna *with Cranberry Steak Sauce and Grilled New Potatoes*
(Serves 6)

FOR THE POTATOES

2 pounds red-skinned new potatoes,
   the smallest you can find
2 tablespoons olive oil
Salt and freshly ground pepper to taste

FOR THE TUNA

6 yellowfin tuna steaks (5 to 6 ounces each;
   ask your fishmonger to cut them thick), or
   1 large piece of yellowfin tuna (2½ to 3 pounds total)
Salt and freshly ground pepper to taste
About 1 tablespoon olive oil
1 recipe Cranberry Steak Sauce (recipe follows),
   warmed
Zest of 2 lemons (4 to 6 teaspoons)

Prepare a mesquite grill for cooking by soaking mesquite chips in water for 1 hour, then adding them to the grill with the regular charcoal.

Grill the potatoes: Put the potatoes and olive oil in a mixing bowl, season with salt and pepper, and toss lightly to coat the potatoes. If the grill is not very clean, wrap the potatoes in aluminum foil.

When the flames of the mesquite coals have died down and just the glowing embers remain, arrange the potatoes in the grill, about 2 inches away from the coals so they don't get direct heat, and cover the grill with a lid, if you have one. Cook the potatoes, turning every 15 minutes, until they are soft all the way through, 30 to 45 minutes total. Move them to the perimeter of the grill to keep warm while you prepare the fish.

Grill the tuna steaks: When the potatoes are done, stir the coals to get the fire going again. Season the tuna steaks with salt and pepper and lightly brush them with the oil. Place the steaks on the hottest part of the grill and cook until marked on the bottom. Flip the tuna over and sear the other side. Keep flipping the tuna until it's cooked to the desired degree of doneness—4 to 6 minutes for small steaks or 8 to 10 minutes for a large one. Be careful not to remove the fish too early; the center should be opaque.

Pour a pool of the steak sauce onto each of 6 dinner plates. Slice each tuna steak and arrange the slices on top of the sauce. Sprinkle the tuna with the lemon zest and serve the potatoes on the side.

Cranberry Steak Sauce
(Makes about 6 cups)

1 small Spanish onion, diced
4 cloves chopped garlic
One 8-ounce can peeled tomatoes
2 cups unsweetened dried cranberries
2 cups cranberry juice
Pinch cayenne pepper
Pinch chili powder
¼ cup coffee
1 tablespoon Worcestershire sauce
1 tablespoon sherry vinegar
Salt to taste

In a saucepan, cook the onion and garlic over medium heat until translucent but not browned, 3 to 5 minutes. Coarsely chop the tomatoes and stir them in, along with their liquid and the dried cranberries. Simmer until the liquid is reduced by half, about 45 minutes. Add the cranberry juice and simmer for 30 minutes more, stirring occasionally.

Remove from the heat and stir in the cayenne pepper, chili powder, coffee, Worcestershire sauce, and vinegar. Puree the mixture in a blender and season with salt. The sauce can be refrigerated for 12 hours or overnight and reheated before serving, if desired.

Cranberry Bread Pudding
with Bourbon Caramel Sauce
and Spiced Pecans
(Serves 6 or more)

1½ loaves Portuguese sweet bread
1¼ cups unsweetened dried cranberries,
  plus more for serving
6 large eggs
2 cups heavy cream
1 cup milk
½ cup sugar
1 tablespoon vanilla extract
2 teaspoons cinnamon
½ teaspoon freshly grated nutmeg

TO SERVE
1 recipe Bourbon Caramel Sauce
  (recipe follows), warmed
1 recipe Spiced Pecans (recipe follows)
Vanilla Whipped Cream (recipe follows)

Remove and discard the crust from the bread. Cut the bread into 1-inch cubes and dry them on the countertop for at least 1 hour.

Preheat the oven to 300° F.

Put the bread cubes in a mixing bowl and sprinkle with the 1¼ cups dried cranberries. In another bowl, mix together the eggs, heavy cream, milk, sugar, vanilla, cinnamon, and nutmeg. Pour the mixture over the bread and cranberries and let sit for 15 minutes to allow the bread to absorb the liquid.

Transfer the soaked bread to a round 10-cup baking dish or 6 small ramekins and bake until the pudding is golden brown on top and the sides have begun to pull away from the dish.

Pour a pool of the caramel sauce on each individual serving plate. Scoop portions of the bread pudding from the baking dish and place it top side up in the pool of sauce. Sprinkle with the nuts and additional dried cranberries and top with the Vanilla Whipped Cream. Serve warm.

Bourbon Caramel Sauce
(Makes about 1½ cups)

1 cup sugar
⅓ cup heavy cream
1 tablespoon unsalted butter
2 tablespoons bourbon
1 tablespoon cider vinegar

Soak a pastry brush in cold water.

In a small saucepan with high sides, combine the sugar and ¼ cup water over medium heat. As the mixture becomes hot, use the pastry brush to brush the inside of the pan so that no crystals form around the edges. Stop brushing the sides of the pan when the mixture starts to boil and forms a clear syrup, in 7 to 10 minutes.

Continue to cook, stirring constantly, until the syrup turns a dark color, 5 to 7 minutes. Remove from the heat and let the syrup cool for 10 minutes. Add the cream to the syrup, then the butter, stirring constantly until the butter is fully incorporated. Stir in the bourbon and vinegar; serve warm.

Spiced Pecans
(Makes about ½ cup)

2 tablespoons sugar
½ teaspoon cinnamon
½ teaspoon ground allspice
⅓ teaspoon ground ginger
1 tablespoon unsalted butter
½ cup pecans, halved

Preheat the oven to 350° F.

In a saucepan over medium heat, combine the sugar, 3 tablespoons water, the cinnamon, allspice, ginger, and butter. Simmer until the mixture thickens, about 5 minutes.

Combine the nuts and the sugar mixture in a mixing bowl, stirring until the nuts are well coated. Pour the mixture onto a small baking sheet or baking dish—they should be in one layer— and bake until the nuts are golden brown, about 10 minutes. Let cool, then break the pecans apart. They can be kept in the refrigerator for 12 hours or overnight before serving, if desired.

Vanilla Whipped Cream

1 cup heavy cream, chilled
1 teaspoon vanilla extract
3 tablespoons sugar

With a chilled whisk, whip all the ingredients together in a copper bowl or chilled stainless steel bowl until soft peaks form. Serve immediately.

peaches-and-herbs anniversary party

In *Gone with the Wind*, Rhett Butler wears an enigmatic smile as he turns from Scarlett O'Hara for the last time. Perhaps he's glad to be rid of her; or perhaps he's looking forward to the delightful evenings he will soon be spending in his hometown, Charleston, South Carolina. Who can blame him? Charleston is arguably the only city as elegant and charismatic as Rhett Butler himself. The people exude a cool Southern charm that is somehow both mannered and laid-back; the streets are lined with brightly painted, historic homes; and the skyline is punctuated by sensual magnolia trees, magnificent oaks, and towering palmettos.

The state motto of South Carolina is "Prepared in mind and resources," and every Southern home in which I've been a guest has embodied it. A pitcher of sun tea is always steeping on the windowsill, and the peaches are picked and ready to slice for the unexpected guest. This is the effortless formality of the South, and I try to bring a measure of it to every party I throw, no matter where I am.

While the soft breezes off the Ashley and Cooper Rivers keep the gardens of Charleston temperate year-round, September is a truly magical time here. Summer has ended with the picnics of Labor Day, and autumn will not officially arrive until the end of the month.

CALL IT INDIAN SUMMER, or call it the last time of the year that you can entertain on your porch with wicker chairs, mint juleps, and the best of your summer garden. The hydrangeas are still abundant, and the rose bushes are fat with richly colored buds: The centerpiece is ready.

I've come to Charleston in September to celebrate the silver anniversary of David and Nell, a pair of Charleston (born and bred!) lovebirds who married twenty-five years ago on September 28TH. The Wrights hired me to help them put together a formal dinner party for thirty friends and relatives at their gracious home on the Battery. Because so many of these folks would be traveling from all over the country, David and Nell really wanted to deliver a party worth crossing many bridges to attend. Not to mention that twenty-five years together is a commitment worthy of great celebration. Nell felt strongly that we use silver, lace, and formal settings, but was concerned about the lingering summer heat, and ways in which they might personalize the affair. Immediately I suggested a cool color scheme for the heat; the use of their wedding gifts, heirlooms, and family photographs to make it theirs; and attention to small details (such as pressed flowers and teacups filled with small bouquets) to add a homespun charm to an otherwise elegant, stately décor.

Before meeting the hosts in person, I expected a couple as formal as the party they described. I've been to my share of cotillions, and as much as I love to feel the nervous energy of a room full of hoop-skirts and crew-cuts, I was relieved to find David and Nell casually waiting for me on their back porch, snapping peas for dinner that night. I began pulling lace samples, ivory place cards, and sachets of fresh lavender from my suitcase, but Nell told me to drop everything and "come on in from the sun."

As Nell led me through their house in her gardening clogs, rummaging through cabinets and drawers, she had a story for every china plate and an eccentric relative for every inherited piece of silver. (I made a mental note to seat Aunt Bunny a good distance from the bar!) While poring over Nell's collection of dishes, we came across the Tiffany-blue salad plates she reserves for serving vine-ripened, sliced tomatoes sprinkled with sea salt, a mixed-matched set of floral-patterned dessert plates for her signature blueberry cobbler ("It's really a compote," she whispered), and her mother's Thanksgiving place settings which she absolutely, as God is her witness, will never take out any other day of the year.

Finally, we came across a pristine tower of cream-colored plates with a lavender and peach floral design. We stopped looking. If you weren't on the receiving end of your family's porcelain fortune, or you haven't been trolling eBay for antique dishes, don't fret! With the exception of Nell's fabulous china, this party was built from scratch. Using the warm glow of peach tones, the soft, cooling hue of lavender, and the dignified polish of silver, I've tried to capture not only a distinctly Charlestonian palette, but the twilight fade of a September evening, and the bright luster of a love that has lasted for many, many years.

A Perfectly Peachy Late Summer Menu

The Wright family, like most Southern families, takes their home cooking very seriously. When it came time to discuss the menu, Nell pulled out her massive collection of inherited recipes and clippings and began poring over it for anything involving peaches. The cheerful sweet peach is South Carolina's state fruit. It is also a staple of Southern cuisine, used in everything from pork roasts to cobblers. Down here they are succulent and grow in abundance, and turns of phrase such as "Why she's as pretty as a peach!" and "He's just peachy," are evidence of Southerners' love for this juicy delight.

Nell insisted that no Southern party is complete without a few delectable tributes to the peach, so together we got to work planning a late summer peach-perfect menu. Her enthusiasm and treasure chest of Southern cooking wisdom convinced me that an outside chef was not necessary. All we needed was a good in-house cook who would understand how to execute Nell's dream menu. In the end, with the help of her nephews (aspiring chefs themselves), the entire feast stayed within the family. Once the menu was resolved, I turned my attention to the presentation, inspired by some ideas I'd gleaned from dining at the Peninsula Grill at Planters Inn—a four-star restaurant that is my favorite place to go whenever I'm in Charleston. What could be more appropriate for this party than home cooking served up in a formal and fanciful style?

We kicked the night's menu off with Shrimp and Peach Kebobs with Fresh Peach Salsa. The kebobs combined large Gulf shrimp with chunks of sweet Vidalia onions and South Carolina peaches. Every bite was an explosion of the sweet and savory. Befitting the formality of the occasion, Nell proposed a main course of her favorite pecan-encrusted rack of lamb with a side of grilled peaches. This succulent dish was a huge success and lovely for late summer, as it can be served hot, warm, or even cool. For dessert, we served the aptly named Peach Dream, a creamy confection presented in individual parfait glasses. This last dish came with a fresh round of Champagne for toasting the happily married couple.

A Silver Anniversary Invitation

Your invitation should capture the elegant but intimate atmosphere and it should, by the look of it, herald the party. Much like a good table setting, layering is the big secret to creating the beauty of a formal invitation. Here, I simply use four layers of alternating white and lavender card stock, each one slightly larger than the next.

Add dimension and texture by attaching a border of white lace (as a reminder of the wedding celebration). Have the party information professionally printed, or write it by hand in a looping cursive script. A calligraphy pen filled with lavender ink makes a striking impression. (But don't be frightened to let your handwriting show your personality!) A traditional invitation reads as follows:

David and Nell Wright
Request the pleasure of your company
for cocktails and dinner
in celebration of their
Twenty-fifth Anniversary
Saturday, September 28, 2002
At seven o'clock in the evening
Eleven Murry Avenue
The Battery
Charleston, South Carolina

Lavender Table Settings

A table setting should be as practical as it is fanciful—after all, this is the battleground of the meal. I love Battenburg lace and use it constantly because it's sturdy, crisp, and easy to care for (unlike Chantilly lace, for example). It has large, striking patterns that work nicely in most settings, and are not too feminine for most situations.

First cover your round tables with lavender bengaline tablecloths. Any medium-weight fabric works well as a substitute; it's the light, lavender color that matters most. Top tablecloths with Battenburg lace overlays. Scatter dried and pressed hydrangea blossoms over the tables and on the silver serving trays to add a delicate splash of color.

Simple Place Cards: We're in the South, so why not enjoy the gentility of place cards? I made these cards with the same paper that I used for the invitations: lavender and white card stock. The design is very simple—for details, see page 155—it's the gesture that adds to the charm of this dinner.

Lace-Backed Chairs: You may not think that your choice of chairs could have such an impact on your décor but they can make the difference between a truly distinctive party design and a "rented" affair. Luckily, you can have it both ways. I transform standard (and rented) Chivari chairs into positive thrones. And all I use are lace place mats and a touch of organza ribbon.

Tie two Battenburg lace place mats to each chair (one to the front and one to the back) with bows of sheer, organza ribbon. Voilà! The charm and individuality of custom chairs.

Glasses: Lavender-hued champagne and water glasses with etched floral designs are a perfect complement to your finished table setting. Crystal is also nice when entertaining with a Southern flair, as are antique glasses in various pastel hues.

Lace Napkins: Each simple Battenburg lace napkin is tied with an antique silver napkin ring and a cluster of dried fresh lavender. If you don't have a cupboard full of antique silver, don't despair: Tie a tiny bundle of lavender to each napkin with a length of your organza ribbon.

Plates: When choosing your plates try to match them to the color motif of your décor. The design on these plates echoes the design of the floral centerpiece. (God is in the details, as every good Southerner knows!) But, there's always an alternative: Arrange pressed hydrangea blooms between a glass plate (on top) and larger white china plate (on bottom) for a simple floral motif!

A Southern-Styled Place Card Table

A striking place card table introduces guests to the fun, herbal twist of this otherwise formal and Southern dinner. For this occasion, the tone is set by fresh and pressed pink and blue hydrangea blooms, bunches of fresh lavender, ribbons of lavender organza, silver picture frames, peach spray roses, and touches of pale yellow yarrow.

- Attach hydrangea blossoms (with florist pins) to the base of a lavender bengaline tablecloth to create a living floral border. If hydrangea grows naturally in your garden, this is a wonderful and inexpensive way to dress up a table.

- Drape six lengths of sheer, lavender organza ribbon across the table (intersecting in the middle, as if slicing a pie) to create a star pattern. I like to use ribbon with wire trim (sometimes referred to as French wire trim), which allows you to shape the ribbon. It's easy to find, inexpensive, and it makes all the difference to the overall look of the party.

- To keep the ribbons from blowing or sliding around, attach tiny bundles of fresh lavender to the ends of the ribbon with pretty bows of matching organza.

- For the final (and functional) touch, arrange the place cards on a three-tiered, silver sandwich stand and surround the base with a wreath of hydrangeas, spray roses, lavender sprigs, and yarrow.

Pressing Issues:
The Art of Pressed Flowers

Using pressed flowers is such a simple and stunning way to add a personal touch to your décor. You can scatter them on tables, attach them to invitations, or toss them at a bride and groom. They make a lovely addition to an end-of-summer party, when every last blossom in your garden can be preserved and enjoyed. And if you had a flower press as a child you know just how easy this technique is.

• Gently remove blooms from stems (try not to handle the petals too much—they bruise easily), and place them between two pieces of parchment paper.

• Slip these flower "sandwiches" between the pages of a large book (a phone book, for example).

• Weigh down the book with a heavy object and let it sit for two or three days.

• Remove the pressed flowers and allow them to dry naturally for a few hours.

Lavender Potpourri

What could be better than walking into a room filled with the alluring scent of a homemade lavender potpourri? Lavender sachets are easy to make and even easier to use. Place sachets or brimming bowls of loose lavender in the powder room, the parlor, even the pantry. However you display these aromatic herbs, the subtle flourish will carry the atmosphere of the party into every room of your home.

• When I make lavender potpourri I add larkspurs, hydrangeas, spray roses, and regular roses.
• Pick your herbs and flowers and hang them by a window for a few weeks until they dry.
• Gently break the flowers and lavender blossoms from their stems and place in a bowl or sachet.

To complement the smoky hue of dried lavender, display your potpourri in a pastel-colored bowl, perhaps a mossy green or a rich plum.

Cranberry-Orange Iced Tea
(Serves 6)

3 orange-flavored tea bags
3 cranberry-flavored tea bags
1 gallon boiling water
1 cup orange juice
1 cup cranberry juice
Springs of fresh mint

1. Add the tea bags to the boiling water in a big glass jar or pitcher and let steep for 10 minutes.
2. Discard the tea bags, then stir in the orange juice and cranberry juice and chill for 2 hours.
3. Serve over ice, garnished with mint sprigs.

Sun Tea with Lemons
(Serves 6)

6 black tea bags
1 gallon cold spring water
Large lemon wedges
Sprigs of fresh mint

1. Add the tea bags to the spring water in a big glass jar or pitcher and let steep in a sunny spot for 2 to 3 hours.
2. Serve over ice, garnished with lemon wedges and plenty of fresh mint sprigs.

Southern Iced Tea

Down South, a concoction of freshly brewed iced tea is never complete until a large quantity of granulated white sugar is stirred into the mix. I make these great tea recipes without sugar, but if you're planning on serving these brews below the Mason-Dixon line, make sure there's a sugar bowl within reach.

Lavender Tea
(Serves 6)

6 black tea bags
1 gallon cold spring water
6 tablespoons fresh lavender
Sprigs of fresh lavender

1. Add the tea bags to the cold spring water in a big glass jar or pitcher.
2. Scoop 3 tablespoons of the fresh lavender into a cone-shaped coffee filter and tie it closed with string. Make another packet of lavender, and add them both to the jar.
3. Place the pitcher in a sunny spot and let steep for 2 to 3 hours.
4. Serve over ice, garnished with lavender sprigs.

Three E's

Essentials
- Hydrangea Floral Border
- Fresh Lavender Bundles and Potpourri
- Peaches

Extras
- Miniature Calla Lilies, Silver Woven Basket
- Silver Picture Frames
- Battenburg Lace Chair Backs and Overlays

Extravagances
- Silver Candelabra, Silver Champagne Stands
- Antique China Plates and Teacups
- Custom Printed Invitations, Framed Table Cards

TUTERA TIPS

- Frame each table card in a unique silver picture frame. To make the table card, find a pretty script font on your computer and print on white stock paper.

- If you don't have a three-tiered sandwich stand, create a similar effect with three matching serving plates or trays (increasing in size from top to bottom), separated with short silver candlesticks. Hot glue the candlesticks to the trays for stability.

- A great trick for putting your smaller buds and blossoms to use is to create a miniature arrangement in an antique porcelain teacup. Here I've used yarrow, raspberry thistle, spray roses, and celosia.

- Lavender works well as a garnish for mashed potatoes or red meat, or slipped into a bundle of asparagus tied with lemon grass.

- Add a sprinkle of lavender to the top of sugar cookies before baking.

- When it comes to scented candles, one small votive candle in the corner of each room will do the trick. Avoid using scented candles at the dining table; the perfume can overwhelm the aroma of the food.

- Add dried, loose lavender blossoms to a small round tin of talcum powder, and you've created a sensual body powder.

- At the end of your party you will want to climb into a perfect bed. For real luxury, add a splash of lavender water to your iron before pressing your pillowcases.

- When storing your sterling silver flatware between uses, wrap it with plastic wrap to help prevent tarnish.

- If you don't have a complete set of colored glassware, you can set each place setting with just one colored glass for splash.

So Long, South Carolina

As I was pulling out of David and Nell's neighborhood for the last time, I nearly had a heart attack when I saw what I thought was a parking ticket. How could I have gotten a ticket? I had been parked in the driveway all night! I swerved to the side of the road and snatched the offending notice from my windshield wiper. But, much to my surprise, this was no ticket; this was a handwritten recipe from Aunt Bunny. Now I know how to make the perfect sloe gin fizz. As I added Aunt Bunny's stellar recipe to my collection of Wright family gardening tips, "perfect" recipes, and "crucial" secret ingredients, I realized that even though I threw the party, I was the one leaving with all the favors. Southerners consider entertaining a gift they give to one another, and in the spirit of Charleston, here's one final gift for you.

Aunt Bunny's Sloe Gin Fizz

1½ ounces sloe gin
2 tablespoons fresh lemon juice
1 teaspoon confectioners' sugar
Splash peach schnapps
6 ounces club soda or to fill
Lemon twist

1. Put the sloe gin, lemon juice, confectioners' sugar, peach schnapps, and plenty of ice cubes in a cocktail shaker.
2. Shake well and strain into a Collins glass filled with ice.
3. Top with club soda and garnish with the lemon twist.

Shrimp and Peach Kebobs
with Fresh Peach Salsa
(Serves 6)

*24 large shrimp, shells and heads left on,
    antennae removed (see Note)*
1½ large Vidalia onions, cut into 2-inch cubes
1½ red bell peppers, cut into 2-inch cubes
*3 ripe but firm peaches, peeled and
    cut into 2-inch cubes*

TO SERVE
1 recipe Fresh Peach Salsa (recipe follows)

Soak 12 bamboo skewers in water for at least 1 hour. Skewer the ingredients onto the bamboo, alternating shrimp and onion, pepper, and peach pieces.

If you are using an outdoor grill, prepare a medium-hot fire. To test the temperature, hold your hand 6 inches above the grill grate: You should be able to count to 3 to 4 seconds before it becomes uncomfortable. If you can only count to 1 or 2, the grill is too hot.

Cook the kebobs on the grill or in a grill pan (if you're using a pan, you will have to work in batches) until the shrimp are firm and pink, 5 to 7 minutes. Serve 2 kebobs per person with the salsa on the side.

NOTE: Grilling shrimp with the head and shell on preserves the flavor, but peeled shrimp can be used if you prefer.
(see photograph, page 162)

Fresh Peach Salsa
(Makes about 2 cups)

1 small Vidalia onion, diced
1½ tomatoes, seeded and diced
3 ripe peaches, peeled, pitted, and diced
1½ teaspoons minced fresh cilantro
1½ tablespoons olive oil
1½ tablespoons red wine vinegar
¾ teaspoon ground cumin
*1 habañero chile pepper, seeded and
    finely minced, or to taste*
Salt and freshly ground pepper to taste

Combine all the ingredients except the salt and pepper in a nonreactive bowl and toss until well coated. Set aside at room temperature until serving time.

Just before serving, season with salt and pepper; adding the salt too early will cause the vegetables to release their natural moisture, resulting in a watery salsa.

Nell's Favorite Rack of Lamb *with Grilled Peaches*

(Serves 6)

3 frenched racks of lamb, chine bone
*   removed (about 3 pounds total)*
Salt and freshly ground pepper to taste
¾ cup finely chopped pecans
1½ tablespoons olive oil
9 ripe peaches (about 2¼ pounds),
*   peeled, halved, and pitted*
1 cup sugar

Preheat the oven to 450° F.

Cut the racks in half, liberally season them with salt and pepper on both sides, and cover them thoroughly with the pecans. Heat a large flameproof roasting pan over medium-high heat, add the oil, and sear the lamb racks until nicely browned on all sides, taking care not to scorch the nuts. (Crowding the pan will cause the pan to cool too rapidly, so sear the racks one at a time.) Transfer the pan to the oven and roast the lamb until it is cooked to your liking, 6 to 8 minutes for medium-rare.

While the lamb is cooking, roughly chop 3 of the peaches and combine them in a nonreactive saucepan with the sugar and 1 cup water. Cook over medium heat until the mixture is reduced by about half, 3 to 5 minutes. Remove from the heat and set aside. (Be careful: The glaze is very hot and sticky.)

Cut the remaining 6 peaches into slices about ½ inch thick and place them on a paper towel to leach out some of the moisture. (Excess moisture will inhibit proper browning.) Grill the peach slices on a medium-hot grill just until the fruit begins to soften, about 2 minutes per side.

As soon as the lamb racks are done, brush them with the warm peach glaze, arrange them on top of the grilled peaches, and serve.

Peach Dream

(Serves 6 or more)

¾ cup sugar
¾ cup egg yolks (from 7 or 8 large eggs)
1 cup heavy cream, chilled
1 tablespoon peach schnapps
2 tablespoons Michele Chiarlo Nivole
  or other good dessert wine
6 ripe peaches (about 1½ pounds), peeled, pitted,
  and very thinly sliced
1½ cups graham cracker crumbs
Sprigs of fresh mint

Combine the sugar and egg yolks in the top of a double boiler over barely simmering water, whisking until the mixture has doubled in volume, 12 to 15 minutes. The mixture should be thick enough that you can draw a figure 8 in it with the whisk. As soon as the desired consistency is achieved, set the pan in a larger bowl filled with ice water to cool.

In a chilled stainless steel bowl, whip the heavy cream with a whisk until it forms stiff peaks, then gently fold it into the sugar and egg yolk mixture. Fold in the schnapps and Nivole.

The dessert can be presented individually in wine or parfait glasses, or in a large, clear glass bowl. Either way, arrange the sliced peaches (reserving a few slices for the top) on the bottom of the serving container and cover them with a generous layer of the graham cracker crumbs. Spoon in the peach cream and garnish with the reserved peaches and mint. Refrigerate for about 1 hour. Serve chilled.

October in Dallas

a ranch country wedding

For starters, forget the ballroom; this is ranch country. Deck the barn with too many

roses, fill the trees with dozens of golden lanterns, set the fine gilt china and crystal

al fresco, and the Waldorf Astoria will have nothing on you. Whatever you do, the cardinal

rule of the Texas wedding is to do it big.

Of course, the cardinal rule of any wedding is to begin with the couple and end with

the couple for every decision you make, from the color scheme to the canapés. And it is

this cardinal rule that brought me to Texas in the first place. It began in the way that most

wedding jobs do for me: Carol Anne's mother told her sister-in-law Judy about a

wedding I did in Fort Worth last fall, then Judy told her best friend Evelyn, Alice's god-

mother to give me a call. The wedding receptions I plan may be featured in *Modern*

Bride, *Country Bride* and just plain *Bridal Guide*, but it's the trusty Longhorn wireless that

carries weight for nervous brides in Texas. For such a personal occasion, word of mouth

is everything, and I'm happy to say that it led Alice to me.

When Alice and I first spoke on the phone she betrayed that adorable combination

of nervous modesty and grand vision common to all brides. She wanted her wedding to

Grant, her college sweetheart, to be a tremendous affair in the tradition of great Texas

weddings, but she also wanted it to remain as simple and rustic as her family's farm.

DURING OUR CONVERSATION, I jotted down all the logistics: Two hundred guests, black tie, early October, seated dinner, outdoor ceremony, dancing in the barn. But it was not until the next day, when I opened my email and found two jpeg files from Alice amidst the spam, that I really started scheming. It was these two simple snap-shots that defined my vision of a grand but delicate affair. One picture showed Alice's wedding dress, the other showed the family barn. The dress was exquisitely modern, with clean lines and a subtle but command-ing train. The classic red barn was both epic and iconic against the bold, blue Texas sky, but not without a functional charm. Together they communicated to me exactly what Alice had in mind but couldn't articu-late. A stunning October wedding began to form in my mind.

A Formal
Country Dinner

The food for Alice and Grant's wedding had to be more than divine; a formal dinner served on the grounds of even the most elegant farm absolutely depends on a touch of unadulterated majesty. And so, the cuisine of William Koval—executive chef at the famous French Room in Dallas' Adolphus Hotel, and conjurer of what must be the most extraordinary culinary reveries west of the Mississippi—was the obvious choice. Koval knows only majesty. In fact, I was sitting in the stunning, rococo dining room of his restaurant, admiring the hand-blown Venetian glass chandeliers and the richly colored murals that cover the vaulted ceiling, when the heavenly clouds painted in those murals brought to mind the clouds above Alice's family ranch.

Koval, with whom I've had the pleasure of working more than once, agreed to design the menu, and the resulting feast was as unearthly a pleasure as befit that gorgeous sky. Guests began with a harvest of fresh, natural flavors when a Field Greens Salad with Heirloom Speckled Roma Tomatoes, Asian Pears, and Maytag Blue Cheese in a Sherry-Balsamic Vinaigrette arrived before them. Next, eyes lit up at the sight of a classic Prime Tenderloin of Beef served with a delicate but ceremonious tian of grilled vegetables, Koval's unforgettable Château Potatoes, and a bold Bordeaux Wine Sauce. And let's just say that people made room for the rich, moist Valrhona Guanaja Hot Chocolate Cake that announced the climax of the meal, not to mention the Vanilla Bean Ice Cream and Roasted Pineapple Sauce that melted against it.

Of course, all of this divinity had to mesh with the more down-home, earthy pleasure of Grant and Alice's celebration, so I created two spicy autumn cocktails for the occasion: a concoction of rum and orange curaçao garnished with a cinnamon stick (it bucks only a little more than a bronco); and a mixture of bourbon, lemon, orange bitters, and ginger ale that I like to think of as a Jack and Ginger for the black-tie set. Pair these two warming libations with the following menu (see page 177), which Koval has scaled down to feed six, and you won't be able to tell whether you're in heaven or Texas.

Casual Opulence:
Country Wedding Décor

It was something about the inherent pageantry of a formal Texan affair, combined with the minimal lines of a country barn, that captured the spirit of what Alice was looking for—a kind of casual opulence. I count this lesson as one of the best I've learned about Texas from a Texan. That is, big is only better when you're talking about something special. It doesn't have to scream Dallas to be Dallas; a dramatic circle of wheat stalks is a bold foundation for a tower of autumnal blossoms, but it's natural and spare as well. Likewise, a heavenly bouquet of flowers—worthy of still-life tribute by an Old Master—is brought closer to earth with a simple knot of bailing twine tied around it. When all is said and done, everything grand is made so by thousands of small gestures.

Even though I had a clear idea of how I wanted Alice and Grant's wedding to feel, the specifics came to mind only after I spent a weekend with them at the family ranch. And on Saturday, October 4TH, those specifics materialized in the form of an unforgettable afternoon wedding. Seasonal shades of gold, rust, and

peach made for a warm, autumnal color scheme; matte velvet tempered copper silk trim; mahogany chairs with brown velvet cushions connected the formal place settings to the casual, country setting; and voluminous arrangements of hydrangea and roses atop rusted brown iron alongside iron candelabras helped balance the robust with the refined.

To complement the autumn flowers, the deep ruddy red of the barn, and the glow of an October sunset, I injected shimmers of gold and blankets of amber light throughout the party, from the forks to the floodlights. In the sparkling light of late afternoon, the gold picked up the sunshine, but once nightfall arrived the magic of these accessories really took hold: From the gold trim of the tablecloths, to the rims of the wineglasses and the flicker from candles, the whole reception was beaming with amber rays. All in all, the grand scale of a big Texas wedding emerged directly from an array of tiny, careful details. After all, isn't that what something as epic as marriage is all about? I trust Alice and Grant will notice all the small, beautiful details along their way.

Autumn Flowers
Beneath the Harvest Moon

Choosing the floral arrangement for a two-hundred-person outdoor wedding may seem daunting; it certainly was for Alice. She, like most brides, felt that her basic understanding of flowers was not sufficient for the kinds of decisions she had to make. But once she laid her eyes on an armful of cascading dahlias and a few bundles of copper-hued roses, her anxiety faded away. Flowers, by nature, lift the spirits. In addition, she realized that she didn't have to get an education in floral design in order to plan her wedding. Florists know how to ask the right questions, show you seasonal motifs, and find creative solutions for working within your budget. To get started, you will need to tally the arrangements you desire. For example, will you need a bouquet for the entryway? Will you need a boutonniere for the ring-bearer? Will you line the driveway with potted blooms? Do you need a headpiece? Here's my standard list of basic arrangements, from which you can pick and choose what you deem necessary.

- Bridal Bouquet
- Bridal Headpiece
- Maid of Honor's Bouquet
- Bridesmaids' Bouquets
- Flowers for the Flower Girl to Toss
  (and/or for her headpiece)
- Mothers' Corsages
- Guest Corsages
- Groom's Boutonniere
- Groomsmen's and Best Man's Boutonnieres
- Fathers' Boutonnieres
- Aisle Runner

- Ceremony Arrangements
  (from scattered petals to altar arrangements)
- Entranceway Arrangements
- Bar/Buffet Arrangements
- Place Card Table Arrangements
- Cocktail Table Arrangements
- Dining Table Arrangements
- Bride and Groom Chair Decorations
- Powder Room Arrangements
- Cake Table Decorations
- Throw Away Bouquet

Awash in Amber, Gilded with Gold

After deciding which arrangements you'll need, it's time to think about what regional flowers are in season and select a unifying color theme. For Alice, this meant autumn blossoms and a harvest palette: From the copper leaf on the invitations, to the coral rose on the groom's boutonniere, to the rusty, rouge poppies in the massive table arrangements, one single motif carried though the ceremony, the bridal party, and the reception. In all, the look was explosive and warm, aglow in hues of amber, rose, and gold. We also took advantage of a few non-floral decorative plants such as strands of golden wheat and large fall leaves. You can also consider dahlias, sunflowers, hydrangeas, chrysanthemums, seasonal berries, leaves, gourds and pumpkins, vegetables, wheat, pods, and mosses. Here's the breakdown for Alice and Grant's wedding.

The invitation was printed on a natural card stock with a burnt-orange border and rust type. In an elegant image, a single autumn leaf accented the card and set the tone for the autumnal motif to come. For the bridal bouquet, Alice wanted something very elegant and subtle to match her simple, stunning dress. We decided on a pretty bouquet of copper-colored roses, mini calla liles (which added a touch of white and sensual curves to the bouquet), as well as a few sprigs of kangaroo paw. Our most lavish feature bouquet was set up on the place card table. This may sound like an odd place for a features tower of blossoms, but keep in mind that this table also served as the "entrance" table. Perched in the center of a sphere of fanned wheat, we filled a rusted, woven-iron urn with moss, roses, hydrangeas, poppies, and dramatic, spindly branches. The effect was phenomenal. And once the coral place cards covered the surface, the look was completed.

In the barn, we accessorized smaller cocktail tables with bundles of wheat, roses, and calla lilies surrounded by pretty green stalks of asparagus and tied with twine. Into each coral napkin, I slipped a small bundle of wheat. If you'd rather choose a loose bridal bouquet, combine long spiky flowers (veronica, upright amaranthus, larkspur) with full round flowers (dahlias and roses) and use soft heads of colorful (blue, lavender, burgundy, green) hydrangeas to create the shape. Tie with a wide ribbon and let the streamers flow.

For the bridesmaids, we created tight bouquets of beautiful roses in warm tones (gold, orange, rust, copper, and coral), accented with pods. We collared the nosegay with galax and other small flat leaves. For the Maid of Honor, we made a stunning bouquet to complement the bridal bouquet: It was made up of orange Unique roses, dark red kangaroo paws, and rust calla lilies, and wrapped with copper ribbon. If you want a non-floral bouquet, try wheat (it symbolizes fertility!) with safflower, orange lanterns, and autumn leaves.

Shiver My Timbers:
What to Do with a Sudden Cold Front?

October is one of my favorite months for weddings. The rich colors, crisp evenings, and dramatic sunsets are unforgettable. In most of America, however, there is a risk of chilly and brisk weather, so be prepared! I had set up tables inside the ranch house, just in case there was a turn in the temperature. I also rented electric heaters (they are much safer than heat lamps, especially when in a barn setting). The bottom line is, always be prepared for bad weather. Even if you are receiving weather reports with a 25 percent chance of rain, make sure you are completely covered with tenting everywhere. Marquee tents, those which connect larger tents, are very, very important. Alice kept telling me not to worry, but when I looked at her stunning Michelle Roth wedding dress and imagined a muddied hem, I got on that Texas longhorn and reserved back-up marquees. Also, remember to put down a carpet runner connecting the areas of an outdoor wedding. The ladies' pumps and heels will thank you!

A wedding tent is a great idea for a large country wedding or an at-home wedding, whether it rains or not. For Alice and Grant, I opted for the barn (it was very clean and dramatic). But I often work with tents for weddings, and the key to fashioning stunning tent décor is to distract attention from poles and supports with colorful and sweeping decorations. Try these ideas:

- Cover central and side poles with beautiful, twisty branches filled with red, rust, and yellow-colored leaves, this will immediately add texture and color.
- The white, vinyl ceiling can be bathed with lighting in warm tones—ambers, golds, and reds with hints of orange.
- Disguise exterior supporting pegs with large, heavy ceramic flower pots filled with orange mums.
- Use numerous long stretches of copper-hued chiffon or tulle to wrap supporting poles, or even to drape Tarzan-vine style from one pole to another.
- Line the tent entrances with vines, ivy, and small orange flowers to create an autumnal archway.
- For bouquets, try these autumn flowers: Dahlias in bright and deep colors like gold, orange, and eggplant; interesting pods for texture; copper-colored hanging amaranthus; sunflowers and Viking mums; celosia (cockscomb) in velvety curls of orange, gold, and red.

Here Comes the Bride, Right on Time

The timeline for Alice and Grant's wedding was planned in advance (it's one I've used before with great success). Here's how we did it:

5:00 PM	Guests are greeted with passed hot cider and sparkling water.
5:30 PM	Ceremony (and sunset) begins.
6:15 PM	Cocktails are passed.
7:15 PM	Guests move to the dining area for dinner and dancing.
11:00 PM	Dessert is served.
12:00 AM	Midnight snacks arrive for the late-night dancing guests.

The First Dance as a Married Couple

Alice and Grant opted for classical guitar for cocktails and a live band for dinner. Later, when the DJ came on, the music of Shania Twain and Garth Brooks could be heard floating up into the night sky. They kicked off the dancing with one of my favorite songs; I may have squeezed out a tear—I know I gasped a little too loud—during "Breathe" by Faith Hill.

Faith Hill	"Breathe"
Faith Hill	"This Kiss"
Don Henley	"Taking You Home"
Shania Twain	"You're Still the One"
Trisha Yearwood	"How Do I Live"
Garth Brooks	"To Make You Feel My Love"
Vince Gill	"I Still Believe in You"
Bob Seger & Martina McBride	"Chances Are"
John Michael Montgomery	"I Love the Way You Love Me"

Please Be Seated

For a two-hundred-person wedding reception, assigned seating, though sometimes complicated to work out, is a really good idea. Aside from the matter of how to match up like-minded guests, the real fun comes in the creative ways you can display place cards. Since we're in the country, here are a few harvest-themed ideas:

- Cut sunflowers flush and pin the card onto the face of the flower.
- Make an incision in a small section of rope or cord, and slip the card into it.
- Tie Indian corn with twine and slip the card into the bow.
- Tie a card to a small section of a twisty manzenita branch (as seen on one of the tables with the crystals).
- For place card retrieval, tie them to the low-hanging branches of a fabulous tree.
- Attach cards to small bundles of dried wheat.
- Pin cards to apple- and pear-shaped candles (these can be lit later on). Place matching real apples and pears in bushels in the middle of the table.
- Make cards out of thin bark paper (available in art and craft stores).
- Take autumn-colored maple leaves and press them flat; with a paint pen write the name of the guest onto the front of the leaf and the number of the table on the other side.
- Punch a hole in the top of a place card and tie a cinnamon stick to it.

The Art of the Wedding Toast

A wedding toast seems like a simple affair, but for some it can be a source of anxiety. Whether you're the best man, best friend, sibling, or parent, your heart will inevitably flood with strong feelings that could leave you speechless. The truth is, the wedding toast is tricky. You are called upon to speak about such grand notions as undying love and yet keep the whole thing funny, accessible, and personal. What to do? Perhaps the best advice I've heard is this: Do not try to sum everything up. Let yourself off the hook a little. All you've been asked to do is lead the guests in a toast to celebrate the couple and their special day.

Autumn Bliss

1 ounce elderberry syrup
4 ounces Moët & Chandon White Star Champagne

1. Put the syrup in a champagne flute, then add the champagne.
2. Give it a gentle stir before serving.

Bourbon Fizz

1½ ounces bourbon
½ ounce fresh lemon juice
2 dashes of orange bitters
2½ ounces ginger ale
Lemon wedge

1. Put the bourbon, lemon juice, bitters, ginger ale, and plenty of ice cubes in a low cocktail glass. Stir.
2. Garnish with the lemon squeeze.

Three E's

Essentials
- Wheat "Bouquets"
- Coral Roses
- Hanging Golden Lanterns

Extras
- Gold-Trimmed Glasses
- Gold Chargers
- Gold-Trimmed Plates

Extravagances
- An Abundance of Calla Lily, Rose, and Hydrangea Arrangements
- Live Classical Guitar and Live Big Band
- Iron Chandeliers

TUTERA TIPS

- For autumn entertaining, create a soup-trio first course: Serve tomato, pumpkin, and potato soup in three separate, hollowed-out gourds set on one plate. It's a wonderful sampling to start off the dinner.

- Create your own place mats or a table runner out of autumn leaves. Simply cut paper to the desired size and glue colorful autumn leaves side by side (start at the edge and overlap your way to the center).

- Use a miniature pumpkin (about the size of a tennis ball) to hold place cards. Simply slice a half-inch-deep incision into the top and slide the place card in.

- Create your own vases. Wrap emptied soup cans with asparagus or cinnamon sticks (or bay leaves glued to the outside) and then tie with raffia. Fill with bittersweet or your favorite flower.

- Line your walkways with little jack-o'-lanterns instead of luminary bags for a festive touch.

- Create a spiral design out of dried wheat to cover the top of a cake table, a place card table, or even the top of cocktail tables.

- For a less formal wedding, create a "surprise seating" for your guests. When they walk from cocktails to dinner, have the male guests draw a card from one bowl and the ladies from another. On each card have the table number—you could end up sitting with your friends or even making new ones.

- Bride tip: A bride should always have a "going away" outfit to change into later in the evening; this way she can be comfortable dancing the night away!

- Create a separate dessert lounge for your guests where you serve dessert wines, chocolate martinis, and coffee.

- Have your bridal bouquet professionally dried—it's worth the expense.

I Left My Heart in Texas

Until the night of Alice and Grant's wedding, I can safely say that I'd never seen so many tuxedos and cowboy boots in one place. But there's no denying that those boots came in handy for the good, old-fashioned line dancing that lasted well into the night. The raucous, foot-stomping climax of the reception, where all the guests joined hands and danced in a circle around the bride and groom to the sound of Johnny Cash's "Ring of Fire," would not have been half as resounding if left to the standard dress shoes and sling-backs. In typical Texas fashion, this wedding was big, bold, and unforgettable; it had both polish and home-style know-how, just like Alice wanted.

When all the dancing was done, I stole a moment to bask beneath the celestial lamp of the big, orange harvest moon. Now, I didn't arrange this particular detail—my connections aren't that good—but it put the finishing touch on this enchanting autumn wedding. Alice and Grant danced for the rest of the night in its ethereal glow, and I knew that from then on, even if they didn't quite know why, a harvest moon would always warm their hearts. And as I watched them together, their eyes filled with love and magic, I realized a small truth that I have tried to keep in mind ever since: No matter how much you plan or fret, in parties as in life, it is often the unexpected that makes a moment last forever. Don't get me wrong, I was secretly proud that the moon cooperated with the warm autumn colors and natural flourishes of this formal party, but it is important to remember that parties belong as much to the instant as they do to design. Alice and Grant were stars, and even that great party planner in the sky could see that much.

October in Dallas
MENU

Courtesy of William Koval, chef of
the French Room at the Adolphus Hotel.

Young Field Greens Salad
with Roma Tomatoes, Asian Pears, and
Blue Cheese in a Sherry–Balsamic Vinaigrette

Prime Tenderloin of Beef
with a Grilled Vegetable Tian, Château Potatoes,
and Red Bordeaux Wine Sauce

Valrhona Guanaja
Hot Chocolate Cake
with Vanilla Bean Ice Cream and
Roasted Pineapple Sauce

Young Field Greens Salad
with Roma Tomatoes, Asian Pears, and
Blue Cheese in a Sherry–Balsamic Vinaigrette
(Serves 6)

2 Asian pears or other juicy pears, peeled and
wrapped in wet paper towels and plastic wrap to
prevent them from turning brown
6 heirloom speckled Roma tomatoes or other plum
tomatoes, blanched (see Notes), peeled, and sliced
into ¼-inch-thick rounds
Salt and freshly ground pepper to taste
6 ounces Maytag blue cheese
12 ounces baby field greens or mixed greens of
your choice, washed and dried (see Notes)
¼ cup Sherry-Balsamic Vinaigrette (recipe follows)

When it's almost serving time, thinly slice the pears using a mandoline or very sharp knife.

Arrange a sliced tomato in a slightly overlapping circle in the center of each of 6 salad plates. Season with salt and pepper, then arrange 3 or 4 slices on pear on top of each tomato circle. Crumble the cheese on top of the pears and tomatoes.

In a nonreactive bowl, toss the greens with the vinaigrette and season with salt and pepper. Arrange the greens on top of the pears and serve.

NOTES: To blanch the tomatoes, make a small X on the bottom of each tomato with a sharp knife. Plunge the tomatoes into a large pot of boiling water for about 8 seconds. Carefully remove them from the water using a slotted spoon and transfer them to a bowl of ice water.

If you wash lettuce in warm water and then refrigerate it, the lettuce will bloom nicely (this works only once).

Sherry-Balsamic Vinaigrette
(Makes 2 scant cups)

1½ tablespoons Dijon mustard
2 tablespoons balsamic vinegar
¼ cup sherry vinegar
2 tablespoons dry sherry
¼ cup tarragon vinegar
1 cup grapeseed oil (available in gourmet food stores)
Salt and freshly ground white pepper to taste

Put the mustard in a nonreactive bowl and whisk in the balsamic vinegar, sherry vinegar, sherry wine, and tarragon vinegar. Gradually add the grapeseed oil, whisking vigorously to make a homogenous mixture. Season with salt and pepper.

Prime Tenderloin of Beef
with a Grilled Vegetable Tian, Château Potatoes, and Red Bordeaux Wine Sauce
(Serves 6)

FOR THE RED BORDEAUX WINE SAUCE
5 shallots, peeled and chopped
2 cloves garlic, chopped
One 750-milliliter bottle red Bordeaux wine
1 bay leaf
1 tablespoon whole black peppercorns
2 sprigs fresh thyme
1 gallon beef stock, preferably homemade

FOR THE BEEF TENDERLOINS
6 prime beef tenderloins or filets mignons
  (8 ounces each)
Salt and freshly ground pepper to taste
1 recipe Grilled Vegetable Tian (page 178)
1 recipe Château Potatoes (page 178)

Prepare a charcoal fire or preheat a gas or stovetop grill to medium-high.

Meanwhile, cook the shallots and garlic together in a heavy-bottom nonreactive pot over medium heat until translucent but not browned. Add the wine, bay leaf, peppercorns, and thyme, and simmer until the liquid is reduced to about ³/₄ cup, about 10 minutes. Pour in the beef stock and simmer until the sauce is reduced to ¹/₂ quart, or to desired consistency, skimming as necessary to remove fat and other impurities—10 to 15 minutes. Strain the sauce through a fine-mesh sieve and keep warm in a saucepan over low heat.

Season the tenderloins with salt and pepper and cook them on the grill for 3 to 4 minutes per side for medium-rare, or to desired degree of doneness. Place one beef tenderloin on each plate and arrange a tian and the potatoes around it. Surround each tenderloin with the sauce and serve immediately.

Grilled Vegetable Tian
(Serves 6)

FOR THE MARINADE
¾ cup extra-virgin olive oil
4 large cloves garlic, minced
6 fresh basil leaves, minced
4 sprigs fresh thyme, minced
3 tablespoons white vinegar
Salt and fresh ground pepper to taste

FOR THE VEGETABLES
12 large portobello mushrooms, at least
   3 inches across (3 to 4 pounds total),
   stems removed, well rinsed, left whole
12 yellow squash, zucchini, or eggplants, or
   a combination (2 to 3 pounds total), trimmed
   and cut lengthwise into ½-inch slices
3 ounces Parmesan cheese, freshly grated

FOR THE TOMATO PASTE
5 large tomatoes (1½ pounds total, peeled,
   seeded, and chopped
2 tablespoons olive oil
Salt and freshly ground pepper to taste

Make the marinade: Whisk all ingredients together in a mixing bowl.

Toss the mushrooms and vegetables in the marinade and let them sit for 1 hour at room temperature.

Meanwhile, make the tomato paste: Place the tomatoes and oil in a skillet or saucepan over low heat and season with salt and pepper. Bring to a simmer and continue simmering, stirring occasionally, until all of the juice has cooked and a paste forms—this should yield about 1½ cups—about 1 hour. Set the tomato paste aside to cool.

Grill the mushrooms and vegetables until tender and cooked all the way through, 3 to 5 minutes on each side. Set aside to cool.

Preheat the oven to 350° F.

Cut the grilled mushrooms into perfect circles so that each fits within a baker's ring; set aside. Dice the mushroom scraps and the other grilled vegetables and transfer them to a mixing bowl; stir in the tomato paste to bind the vegetables together. Stir in the cheese.

Butter 6 stainless steel 3-inch baker's rings 1¾ inches high. Arrange the prepared rings on a baking sheet and place one trimmed mushroom cap, top down, in the bottom of each ring. Divide the vegetable mixture among the rings and top each with a second trimmed mushroom, cap facing up. Bake for 10 to 12 minutes.

Using a spatula, transfer the individual tians, along with the rings, to serving plates. Remove the rings and serve the tians hot.

Château Potatoes
(Serves 6)

2 tablespoons grapeseed oil (available in
   gourmet food stores)
3 large baking potatoes (about 1¼ pounds),
   cut into quarters and thickly sliced
5 sprigs fresh thyme
2 sprigs fresh rosemary
1 clove garlic, chopped
1 tablespoon salted butter
Salt and freshly ground pepper to taste

Preheat the oven to 350° F.

Heat the oil in an ovenproof skillet over medium-high heat. When the oil is hot, add the potato slices. Cook the potatoes until nicely browned on both sides, 3 to 5 minutes, then add the herbs, garlic, and butter, season with salt and pepper, and toss to combine.

Continue cooking the potato mixture in the skillet or transfer it to a baking sheet and bake for 15 to 20 minutes, until the potatoes are soft in the center. Let cool for 10 to 12 minutes before serving.

Valrhona Guanaja Hot Chocolate Cake *with Vanilla Bean Ice Cream and Roasted Pineapple Sauce*

(Serves 6)

¾ cup plus 2 tablespoons unsalted butter,
   plus more for the ramekins
6 tablespoons all-purpose flour, plus more
   for the ramekins
¾ cup plus 2 tablespoons chocolate chips, preferably
   Valrhona or other rich bittersweet chocolate
4 large eggs
4 large egg yolks
¾ cup plus 2 tablespoons confectioners' sugar
¼ teaspoon salt
1 shot amaretto

TO SERVE
Premium vanilla bean ice cream
1 recipe Roasted Pineapple Sauce (recipe follows)

Butter and flour six 8-ounce ramekins.

Heat the chocolate and the ¾ cup plus 2 tablespoons butter in the top of a double boiler over barely simmering water until they're melted, about 5 minutes; set aside.

Beat the eggs and egg yolks together in a nonreactive bowl until smooth, then fold them into the melted chocolate mixture. Sift the 6 tablespoons flour, the confectioners' sugar, and salt together, then fold the flour mixture into the chocolate mixture until just combined. Stir in the amaretto.

Divide the cake batter among the prepared ramekins and let sit for 30 minutes—if the batter has time to settle, the cakes will be richer. Fifteen minutes before baking time, preheat the oven to 450° F. Bake until the tops split, 8 to 10 minutes.

Let the cakes cool for 7 to 10 minutes, then, one by one, turn the ramekins upside down and shake gently to transfer each cake to a dessert plate. Add a small scoop of ice cream and surround each still-warm cake with the pineapple sauce.

Roasted Pineapple Sauce

(Makes about 1½ cups)

½ fresh pineapple, cored and peeled,
   chopped into 1-inch chunks (to yield about 2 cups)
2 tablespoons unsalted butter
¼ cup heavy cream
1 tablespoon sugar
1 shot high-quality rum
   (Myers Rum is a good choice)

Preheat the oven to 400° F.

Spread the pineapple chunks on a baking sheet and roast them 20 to 25 minutes, until soft and browned.

Transfer the roasted pineapple to a blender, add the remaining ingredients, and blend until thoroughly incorporated. Refrigerate the sauce until chilled; you can keep the sauce, covered, in the refrigerator for 12 hours or overnight.

November in Chicago

*a closing night cocktail party
and an urban thanksgiving*

For residents of the Windy City, the arrival of November usually means the first freeze of the year. Fortunately, it also means that the party season is really heating up. Of course, this is true pretty much no matter where you are or what the temperature is. The fervor of the Christmas countdown is yet to come, but the magic is already in the air. Folks are still excited about their fall fashions, the lighting of their first fire, and all the invitations arriving in their mailboxes. The brisk (though not yet brutal) winter weather fills the air with energy, and people keep warm at cocktail parties and around tables laid with oven-cooked meals; the instinct to hibernate is months away!

I love Chicago. Maybe it's the great deep-dish pizza, maybe it's the amazing Mexican restaurants, maybe it's the music pouring out of all the blues clubs. But for my money, the best thing about Chicago is the unflappable spirit of the natives. No matter how bitter the winter, there's always a home fire burning and most likely a party inside. After all, what better way to warm up than with a few cocktails and a little dancing?

November usually finds me planning what seems like a thousand parties. This year I had the pleasure of producing two very different parties in Chicago: not only a sophisticated new interpretation of the traditional Thanksgiving dinner, but also a chic surprise cocktail party for a group of actors celebrating the closing night of a hit play. With all the heat generated by these parties, it's a wonder that winter came at all!

A Closing Night Cocktail Party

The only thing I love more than throwing a great party is throwing a great surprise party, so I was thrilled when an outrageous, wonderful theater director I worked with years ago, asked me to throw one for the actors in his Chicago theater company.

Ted wanted to host a late-night party, but he knew that the impersonal nature of a bar or a restaurant wasn't going to cut it. He preferred a more intimate get-together, where recollections of missed lines, trip-ups, and near disasters could last well into the night, uninterrupted by polite waiters, bar tabs, and that pesky matter of closing time: It had to be at home.

According to Ted, having the party at his spacious Wicker Park loft would also add to the element of surprise. He knew that even the smallest gesture, such as throwing a scarf over a lamp, would impress this crowd. I had bigger plans than that, but Ted was skeptical. "Wait till you see my place," he said, "It's not exactly the lobby of the Four Seasons." Four Seasons or not, I liked the idea of shocking his guests with a completely transformed space. They'd show up prepared for a night among unbound stacks of scripts and open bags of pretzels, only to find themselves in a chic, cozy environment, a place where every effort had been made to provide for their comfort and enjoyment. I saw the Chicago of Al Capone's Prohibition-era days rising before me: a clean color palette of black, white, and navy; jazz and blues records playing late into the night; classic cocktails and simple, elegant bar fare. Creating the modern speakeasy wouldn't exactly be easy, but I knew what I wanted. And hey, I love a challenge.

When I arrived at Ted's warehouse-style building, took the freight elevator up, and pushed open the heavy steel door to his loft, I learned something about him. Though enormous, the place was, well, let's just say it was cluttered. But cluttered in the best sense of the word! All around me was evidence of a brilliant career: play scripts in stacks on dusty bookshelves, set design illustrations pinned to walls, newspaper clippings spilling from a desk drawer. I instinctively scanned the room for a lamp to throw a scarf over.

As soon as I mentioned the possibility of "cleaning up," we both started laughing. This would not be cleaning up, this would be remodeling life. And there was no reason to remodel Ted's life. The apartment perfectly reflected his tastes, his style, and his passion. So I suggested that we simply cover the key areas affected by this "passion." Other than the desk, a few bookshelves, and the walls of clippings, the place was sparingly decorated and refreshingly minimal. There was hope yet. Especially after I found a baby grand piano tucked off in a far corner under a sheet. It was just begging to be unwrapped and dragged to the center of the room! But the real coup came a few days later, when we met at the theater. After snooping around the prop shop for a while in search of inspiration, I was thrilled to find some stage dividers that had been used for a 1930s-gangster-era play he'd directed years ago. Those stacks of papers and clippings vanished from the setting of the party behind plush, ivory leather screens that were straight out of the Paradise Club.

Even if you don't have a theater full of props or a house full of unfiled papers and books, don't underestimate the effect of a transformed space on the guests at your surprise cocktail party. Let your theatrical side come out; put on a play. After all, the Prohibition era (for anyone at a cocktail party, anyway) was all about making the best of your resources and creating an environment that was not what it seemed. And we can all raise a glass to that.

Cocktail Napkin Invitation

Ted was adamant that his actors suspect nothing more was in the cards than a few lukewarm Molson Goldens and an evening set to the same "Blues Greats" records that were sitting on his turntable at the last party; in short, a regular evening with Ted. This made the invitations a little trickier to design: they had to be intriguing and formal enough to be taken seriously, but they also had to appear as if they were truly "dashed-off" at the last minute (like most of Ted's gestures!). A quick handwritten note on a white linen cocktail napkin would hit the right tone. I gave Ted fifteen starched, white napkins folded and pressed into squares. He wrote, in his own inimitable style:

Time to celebrate.
Come on over to my place after the show
And stay until I kick you out!
(Ted's address added here with a funny drawing of his building)
(Ted's signature)

Although I myself had never designed an invitation with the words "kick you out" on it, I had a feeling this one was absolutely perfect. Directors can be so bossy!

Cocktail Décor

The ivory screens I borrowed from the theater really took Ted's party back to the jazz era. But to update the black, white, and silver palette, I used classic blue- and ivory-striped tablecloths, which also create a nice visual echo of piano keys. For the finishing touch, I placed a brandy snifter filled with blue-dyed water and floating gardenias in the center of each table, surrounded by votives made of chrome wire. This arrangement is simple enough not to interfere with the rest of the décor's nostalgic nod to the past, and it's sharp enough not just for the modern day, but more importantly, the modern night.

Spinning Records, Serving Snacks

Serve simple hors d'oeuvres on old vinyl records. Choose a scratched record that no longer plays or a vintage (though not precious!) jazz album. But whatever you do, don't attempt to clean your records in the dishwasher! They'll warp and curl right up. Simply wipe them down with cold water and a little detergent, and dry them with a towel. Then rub a tiny amount of olive oil onto the surface to get that nice black-vinyl sheen. This is one use for those old records that will have guests singing your praises.

Jazz It Up!

My personal favorite cocktail numbers come from the great female crooners of the 1950s: Nancy White, Ella Fitzgerald, Sarah Vaughn, and Peggy Lee. But it's nice to mix the sexy retro sounds of these soulful singers with a few perfectly mellow jazz favorites such as Miles Davis's "Kind of Blue," samba-style Stan Getz CDs (such as Getz/Gilberto with the classic track "Girl from Ipanema" on it), or John Coltrane's "My Favorite Things." Keep in mind that softer jazz collections or piano music are ideal for parties because you can talk over the music. It's a little harder to talk over trumpet and saxophone, unless it's gentle Miles Davis, soothing soprano sax from John Coltrane, or Stan Getz. A Chicago jazz record collector friend of mine once gave me this wonderful tip (listen to the record once, and you'll agree): *Ahmad Jamal/Live from the Pershing Lounge* may just be the ultimate subtle-quite-jazzy-gospel-soulful background CD. Currently two of my favorite CDs are Norah Jones's *Come Away with Me* and Diana Kroll's *The Look of Love* and *When I Look in Your Eyes*. To add a more funky club sound to your party, I absolutely love Hôtel Costes, various volumes.

Cocktail Anyone?

At a casual cocktail party such as this, I think it's absolutely appropriate to let guests help themselves to drinks. A few printed cocktail recipes, however, add just the right dose of formality to a good self-service bar. Place cocktail recipes in small silver picture frames propped up on the bar, and watch the guests have fun making their own drinks! This makes for a wonderful interactive party, and gets folks to experiment a little with all the ingredients, tools, glasses, and garnishes you've so thoughtfully laid out.

Although your guests will be helping themselves at the bar, get them in the spirit by offering them a drink the minute they come in from the cold. Ted's guests were completely blown away when he opened the door wearing a cocktail waiter's apron, with a towel draped over his forearm and a tray of drinks in his hands. There are, after all, few better surprises than the offer of an unexpected Tiffany-Blue Martini.

Tiffany-Blue Martini

2 ounces vodka, preferably Belvedere
¾ ounce blue curaçao
1 ounce pineapple juice
3 blueberries on a cocktail skewer

1. Put the vodka, curaçao, pineapple juice and plenty of ice cubes in a cocktail shaker.
2. Shake well and strain into a chilled martini glass.
3. Garnish with the skewered blueberries.

Black Velvet

4 ounces vodka, preferably Belvedere
2 ounces Chambord
1 ounce blue curaçao
1 large blackberry

1. Put the vodka, Chambord, blue curaçao, and plenty of ice cubes in a cocktail shaker.
2. Shake well, pour into an old fashioned glass, and garnish with the blackberry.

Sidecar

Lime wedge
Sugar in the raw
2 ounces brandy
Juice of ½ lime (about 1 tablespoon)
½ ounce Grand Marnier
Lime twist

1. Moisten the rim of a brandy snifter with the lime wedge and dip the rim of the glass into the sugar.
2. Put the brandy, lime juice, Grand Marnier, and plenty of ice cubes in a cocktail shaker.
3. Shake well and strain into the brandy snifter.
4. Garnish with the lime twist.

Smoky Martini

2½ ounces gin
½ ounce bourbon
Dash dry vermouth
1 black cherry, stem stilled attached

1. Put the gin, bourbon, vermouth, and plenty of ice cubes in a cocktail shaker.
2. Shake well and strain into a chilled martini glass.
3. Garnish with the black cherry.

Classic Cocktail Bar Checklist

Of course, not every one of these gadgets and tools is necessary to make a good martini. In fact, most of the best drinks are often simple and simply made. Having said that, just a skim over this list gives you an idea of all the fun and silvery sparkle a well-equipped bar can bring to a room. Grab what you can, but don't fret if you've got to use a teaspoon in place of a muddler. Your guests will forgive you.

- Sifter
- Pourer
- Shot Glass
- Measures/Jigger
- Paring Knife
- Salt Saucer
- Bar Strainer
- Bar Spoon

- Muddler
- Cocktail Sticks
- Straws
- Mixing Glass
- Cocktail Shaker
- Blender
- Sharp Knife
- Cutting Board

- Ice Bucket
- Tongs for Ice
- Corkscrew
- Lemon & Lime Squeezer
- Hand Towel
- Simple Syrup (see recipe page 39)

Three E's

Essentials
- Jazz
- Specialty Cocktails
- Cocktail Tables and Lamps

Extras
- Complete Bar Set
- Printed Cocktail Recipes
- Printed Cocktail Napkin Invitation

Extravagances
- White Leather Screens
- Vintage Cocktail Cart
- Baby Grand Piano

TUTERA TIPS

- Serve cocktail snacks, such as sweet and spicy almonds, honey-salted cashews, and chopped dates, in martini glasses.

- Burn your favorite jazz songs onto a CD as a gift for your guests. When they put on the CD they'll be reminded of what a wonderful time they had dancing around your baby grand and drinking those sexy blue drinks!

- For a cocktail party with no bartender, get your guests into the act by displaying interesting cocktail recipes in silver frames on the bar.

- Don't shy away from serving something more than finger food at a cocktail party. Just be creative! I cut holes in a wooden tray so that Ted could easily serve shot glasses of cold soup to the guests at his party. It was refreshing, effortless, and perfect for a room full of creative cocktail enthusiasts.

- When making cocktails that call for orange juice or lemonade, always strain the juice first to remove any pulp. Strained juice will allow the cocktail to be more translucent and more elegant.

An Urban Thanksgiving

Everyone's relationship to Thanksgiving changes as they grow up. At age eight, it's all about making turkeys out of construction paper at school, sticking fake pilgrim buckles to your Keds, and the freedom to eat unlimited pie. By the time seventeen rolls around, your thrill comes from sitting at the grown-up table and then hot-footing out to the car to meet friends for a movie. But by twenty-five, things are a little different. Thanksgiving becomes a three-day weekend with your family that you and your therapist have planned for since Labor Day. Yes, the origins of this holiday reside in the more tender moments: breaking bread with others, sharing your home with friends, honoring the peace between

neighbors, and giving thanks for the bounty of life. But let's face it. It's also the ultimate family holiday, and families are complicated. If your needling Aunt Myra isn't criticizing your stuffing, your unemployed cousin Jimmy is packing it up in a doggie bag before it's even been served. Your mother wants to know why you still haven't found that perfect someone, and your father opts for Wild Turkey over dry turkey.

In spite of those long lines at the airport and the overall state of chaos, most of us also relish the time with our families, not to mention the incredible indulgence of a day entirely devoted to eating delicious home-cooked food: We head on home. But if you just couldn't make that last flight out of town and find yourself facing a long weekend of watching TV alone and eating an entire Mrs. Smith's Apple Pie out of the freezer, take heart! There are others out there, and chances are you know a few of them. I definitely know at least one of them: Helen, a Chicago attorney, called me in a panic in early November. Every year she joins her family in San Diego for their big, sprawling feast, but this year she simply could not. Nevertheless, she wanted to make the best of the day by entertaining a group of friends and colleagues in her newly renovated Lincoln Park apartment. This party would be the first in her new dining room, so she wanted it to be fabulous. She loves to cook and entertain, but, always the consummate professional, she also knows when to delegate responsibility. This would be one Thanksgiving where her brother Tom wasn't there to run out for vanilla extract in the final hour. And he wouldn't have to.

On the phone, Helen said that she would love to prepare everything herself, but just couldn't bear to do it without the peanut gallery there to "advise." And with several trials on the calendar, she wanted nothing more than to take a long, hot bath on Thanksgiving morning. There she would give a silent prayer of thanks for her jasmine-scented bath salts and the full eight hours of sleep ahead of her after the feast. When the subject of food came up in our discussion, Helen sighed. She longed for her mother's famous mashed potatoes, but also wanted a party that would feel as young as she did and as modern as her new digs. It was up to me to create both a meal and a setting that were warm but fresh, and traditional but a little spectacular. By the time we said goodbye, jasmine votives and elegant arrangements of orchids were already a given, as far as I was concerned.

Because this Thanksgiving would not be like any other she'd had, I decided to make it completely different. She wasn't going to smell the warm aroma of her mother's apple pie from the kitchen, and she sure wasn't going to sit around in her father's old Barcalounger, so why pretend? It's important to strike out and define your own Thanksgiving. And for Helen, I sensed that this meant something peaceful, modern, and sophisticated; something as soothing as the hot bath she would take the morning of the big event.

Zen and the Art of Turkey Eating

When Helen and her guests finally sat down to their own private Thanksgiving dinner, everything was in place. The warm colors of Thanksgiving had been reincarnated as a simple Japanese-influenced arrangement of smooth stones, white orchids, auburn-colored roasted pomegranates, and tranquil green leaves. And thanks to chef Arun Sampanthavivat, owner of Chicago's Arun's, the traditional cornucopia also took on an Asian accent: The turkey was garnished with mashed taro and cranberry-kaffir lime sauce; the mashed potatoes were spiked with wasabi; hot greens were replaced by a light herb salad topped with pear and orange segments and a subtle Thai ginger dressing; and the all-important pie was not pumpkin, but rather a Thai kabocha squash pie.

Asian cuisine-meets-a-traditional-American Thanksgiving is not typical. And neither is Arun. He didn't even flinch at the idea of these two culinary styles fused together to form what might become a new Thanksgiving tradition. This was truly Zen and the art of turkey eating, and if the tryptophan didn't soothe these edgy urbanities, the multiple rounds of hot sake certainly would.

The Thanksgiving Table

One single runner stretched across a full-length dining room table doesn't always really blow the horn of plenty, if you know what I mean (especially on festive occasions). So for Helen's Thanksgiving table, I sewed two chartreuse green silk runners together to make one bold statement. To bring out the green and highlight each place setting, I rolled plum-colored napkins and stuffed them into napkin rings decorated with plum, red, and green beads. But my big, glamorous splurge for the table was the beautiful selection of hand-blown glasses. The glasses reflected all the warm colors of the autumn season, and of my modern Thanksgiving palette: green-hued red wineglasses, plum-colored white wineglasses, and glowing amber water glasses. I passed sake in small green ceramic cups, but a set of sake cups in any shade of plum, moss green, ivory, or deep orange would look wonderful in this delicate and vibrant setting. For a modern look, simple, white, square-shaped dishes accentuated the clean lines of this table setting and instantly reframed a traditional plate of turkey and cranberry sauce. A hint of bamboo came across in the sculpted handles of the gold flatware. Real bamboo handles can be substituted, or very modern, minimalist knives and forks.

Centerpiece

I love orchids of all colors, but there's nothing quite like classic paper-white *Phalaenopsis* orchids (or "phals"). You will most likely purchase an orchid already potted, so ask for a simple chartreuse container, or repot your orchid when it arrives. Orchids are basically plants that grow on trees. They attach to tree trunks and branches with their roots exposed to the air, and absorb water and nutrients from the air, rain, and whatever drips down the tree. This is the reason why many orchids need to be potted in very porous, well-drained soil that will not hold water easily. Remember: Your orchid can withstand periods of forgetfulness and drought better then it can handle over-watering. When using an orchid for the centerpiece, be sure to cover the exposed soil with a layer of fresh green moss. Not only does this look elegant and beautiful, it also helps the orchid grow.

How to Make Your Orchid Grow

- When you first bring your orchid home give it a good watering. (I have yet to see an orchid in a store that was wet.)
- The best place for watering is probably in the kitchen sink. Run a gentle trickle of lukewarm water for about 15 seconds. Be sure to thoroughly wet the soil.
- Allow the plant to drain for about 15 minutes. (It may appear dry, but it has had enough water.)
- Throughout the course of the week, check your plant to see if it needs water by pushing your finger about one inch into the soil. If it is completely dry, you can rewater.
- Orchids can last for many months, as long as the roots are not soaked and smothered with too much moisture.

Countdown to Turkey Day

Day Seven
• On your way home from work, order a big, fresh organic turkey. I recommend avoiding frozen or pre-basted turkeys. If possible, go for a kosher turkey. They're my all-time favorites and always taste fabulous. You'll need two pounds per person, so for eight people, a 16- to 20- pounder should be just right (this allows for plenty of over-stuffed turkey sandwiches the next day).

Day Six
• Order two white "phal" orchid plants from your local florist, and make sure they are potted in designer pots (in this case, pale green would be ideal). Ask the florist to cover the soil in the pot with a layer of moss and to deliver it in the morning before you leave for work.

Day Five
• Tip the orchid delivery boy when he comes at an ungodly 7:30 AM. Go online or pick up the phone and order your wine from a local wine shop. A selection of zippy Australian shiraz reds or cabernet-shiraz blends is the perfect match for a juicy turkey dinner. Also pick out a few bottles of a crisp Italian pinot grigio for white wine drinkers. Order two bottles of sake; leave one out for heating and pop the other in the fridge.

Zen Palette Color Checklist

GREEN
Runner
Red Wineglasses
Artichoke Candle Holders
Centerpiece Vase and Moss
Beans and Wasabi Potatoes

AMBER
Water Glasses
Dried Pomegranates
Carrots and Ginger

PLUM
Napkins
White Wineglasses
Cranberry Sauce

Day Four
• During your lunch break, hop in the car (or a cab) and head for the closest Asian grocery store (check the Yellow Pages). Have your list of specialty ingredients from the following menu ready.

Day Three
• Freak out because you didn't really buy your turkey on "Day Seven." Run out and pick up a last-minute turkey from the grocery store; one can of gold paint from an art supply store; two fresh artichokes, beans, carrots, ginger, potatoes, and cranberries from the greengrocer; and a dozen breadsticks from the bakery.
• Go home, put slippers on, and set up a workstation in front of the TV. Spread newspaper on the floor, and get your brush out. While watching your favorite drama, carefully paint the tips of your artichokes with gold paint, then set them on the windowsill to dry.

Day Two
• Leave work early. Sneak just one glass of the sake that has arrived and figure out what you're going to wear. Make sure it's comfortable and has the kind of laid-back modern attitude of your table setting.
• Listen to your favorite CD while you brine the turkey, make the wild rice stuffing, and cook the pies.
• Put away any personal items scattered around the house and water your new orchids if necessary.
• Draw up a battle plan for tomorrow. Such as:

Day One
9:30 AM Wake up, put on your favorite T-shirt, and light jasmine candles. Then stuff the turkey and put it in the oven.
10:00 AM Peel and dice potatoes. Place in a bowl of cold water and set aside. Baste the turkey.
10:30 AM Snip the ends off the green beans and peel the pearl onions and carrots.
11:00 AM Take a long shower (or bath!), get dressed, and have a quick sip of sake. Baste the turkey again. Do a final wipe-down of the kitchen and crack a window. Arrange the serving trays and implements.
12:30 PM Baste the turkey. Heat some sake for your soon-to-be-arriving guests, and sample it for quality. Put on some good music and decide that people can take their shoes off at the door. Take your shoes off.
1:00 PM Have one more sip of sake, just to make sure the temperature is perfect, and answer the door.

Three E's

Essentials
- Orchids
- Square Casual China
- Jasmine-Scented Candles

Extras
- Gold-Tipped Artichokes
- Smooth River Stones
- Matching Sake Carafe and Cups

Extravagances
- Hand-Blown Amber, Green, and Plum Glasses
- Gold Bamboo-Shaped Flatware
- Wakatake Daiginjo "Onikoroshi" Sake ($75 per bottle, retail)

TUTERA TIPS

- Cut sections of bamboo (select stalks that are roughly $1^1/_2$ inches in diameter) into 1-inch long sections, then thread rolled napkins through them. Voilà! You've got an elegant set of napkin rings.

- Artichokes are floral, robust, and firm to the touch, so they make wonderful candleholders. Simply push back the inside leaves to create a small hole in the base of the heart (slightly smaller than the diameter of a tapered candle). Use oil-based gold paint, or even gold nail polish, to paint the tips of the leaves. Cut off stems so they sit upright on the table.

- When heating sake, it is important not to let it boil or to let the carafe get too hot to touch. The best way I know to do it is simply to boil water in a shallow saucepan (the water should be about 2 inches high), and then turn off the heat. Place your sake carafes in the simmering water for three to five minutes.

- When making a turkey, it's important not to overcook. Try using a self-basting roaster. Still do your usual basting every thirty minutes, as this allows for extra protection against drying out. General cooking times for an unstuffed turkey:

14 to 18 pounds	$3^3/_4$ to $4^1/_4$ hours
18 to 20 pounds	$4^1/_4$ to $4^1/_2$ hours
20 to 24 pounds	$4^1/_2$ to 5 hours

- Always warm your guests' plates in the microwave before serving. This keeps the food warm, especially when serving buffet style. Simply stack two or three plates and microwave on high for 15 to 20 seconds. If you don't have a microwave, run the plates under hot water and dry quickly.

Our Parties, Our Selves

As I nibbled on my mother's famous apple and sausage stuffing the day after Thanksgiving, the refrigerator door hanging wide open, I imagined how it might taste with Helen's sake-braised turkey. Of course, judging from her email, there wasn't much left for sandwiches. And as far as I could tell, there wasn't much sake left over, either; she reported a wild lightning-round of legal charades that climaxed with her miming of the Taft-Hartley Act (I didn't ask for details). The whole thing was a huge hit, and the case didn't close on this fabulous holiday until everyone had appealed Helen's motion to save the second pie for lunchtime leftovers in the office on Monday.

The news from Ted was equally good. There were no charades for this group—perhaps they got enough of that in rehearsal—but there was, I'm told, a first-rate rendition of Peggy Lee's "Fever," complete with a Bob Fosse dance sequence. In Ted's words, "It was high drama; the fourth wall was never broken, and miraculously, neither were any of the dozens of martini glasses we went through." Since I think of parties as a kind of theatrical improvisation, I took that as a huge compliment.

As I reflected on these two very different parties, I was surprised to realize how much they actually had in common. Ted may be a seasoned veteran of the opening night jitters, and Helen may be a cool litigator, but I received the age-old pre-party S.O.S. from each of them in the minutes before their doorbells rang for the first time. This is perfectly normal. When we entertain at home, we all have the yikes: We are certain that a tiny piece of our personal chaos will intrude on the smooth artifice of the party. But with a few simple touches—a little sake on the turkey, a few chic leather screens for ambiance—we can transform our sense of everyday life so completely that the seeming theater of the party reveals itself as reality. And if you're lucky, you might even win a game of charades.

November In Chicago
MENU

Courtesy of Arun Sampanthavivat, chef of Arun's.

Herbed Salad
with Pears and Orange Segments

Sliced Roast Turkey
with Wasabi-Infused Mashed Potatoes and Cranberry-Kaffir Lime Sauce

Kabocha Pie

Herbed Salad
with Pears and Orange Segments
(Serves 6)

2 cups mixed salad greens
¼ cup fresh mixed herb leaves,
   such as arugula, cilantro, mint, and basil
2 to 3 tablespoons Herbed Dressing (recipe follows)
2 Asian pears or other juicy pears, peeled and
   thinly sliced
2 oranges, peeled, all membranes
   removed from segments

Gently toss the greens, herbs, and dressing together in a mixing bowl.

    Arrange the salad on individual serving plates and top with the pears and orange segments.

Herbed Dressing
(Makes about 1¼ cups)

½ teaspoon finely minced galangal
   (Thai ginger, available at Asian markets)
1 teaspoon fresh lemon grass,
   tough outer layers removed, finely minced
1 teaspoon minced white onion
½ teaspoon finely minced kaffir lime leaves
   (available at Asian markets)
1 cup white vinegar
1 teaspoon salt
2 teaspoons garlic oil or olive oil

Using an electric mixer, blend the galangal, lemon grass, onion, and lime leaves in a nonreactive bowl. Thoroughly blend the vinegar and salt into the herb mixture until the salt is completely dissolved, then add oil and blend again until emulsified.

Sliced Roast Turkey

*with Wasabi-Infused Mashed Potatoes
and Cranberry-Kaffir Lime Sauce*
(Serves 6 or more, with leftovers)

This recipe requires 2-day advance preparation.

1 large turkey (about 18 pounds)
½ cup salt
¼ cup sugar
4 bay leaves
½ shallot, finely minced
4 to 5 cloves garlic, finely minced
1 teaspoon whole white peppercorns
1 recipe Wasabi-Infused Mashed Potatoes
   (recipe follows)
1 recipe Cranberry-Kaffir Lime Sauce (recipe follows)

If the turkey has a metal clamp on its legs, remove it. In a plastic pot large enough to accommodate the whole turkey, combine 8 cups cold water, the salt, sugar, bay leaves, shallot, garlic, and white peppercorns, stirring to dissolve the salt and sugar. Place the turkey in the brine, breast side down, cover the container, and refrigerate for 12 hours or overnight.

Remove the turkey from the brine and transfer it, breast side up, to a roasting pan with a rack. Place it in the refrigerator to dry for 12 hours or overnight. Transfer the brine to a nonreactive bowl and refrigerate it, too.

Preheat the oven to 400° F.

Pour 3 cups of the brine into the bottom of the roasting pan and cover the turkey with a lid or aluminum foil. Roast for 10 to 15 minutes to sear it. Lower the oven temperature to 350° F and roast until done, 4 to 4½ hours for an 18-pound turkey. (Use a meat thermometer to test doneness; the turkey is done when the internal temperature of the thickest part of the thigh is about 170° F.)

When the turkey is fully cooked, remove the lid or foil and return the turkey to the oven at 400° F for 15 to 20 minutes, until the skin is brown. Let the turkey rest for 15 minutes before carving. Serve the turkey, sauce, and mashed potatoes buffet style.

Wasabi-Infused Mashed Potatoes

(Serves 6 or more)

This recipe is one of my holiday favorites.

*2 pounds russet potatoes, peeled and cut
    into 2-inch cubes*
Salt
¾ cup whole milk
1 tablespoon wasabi powder
⅓ cup salted butter
*½ cup crushed wasabi peas (available at
    Asian markets), plus more for garnish*

Place the potatoes in a large pot of cold salted water. Bring the water to a boil and cook the potatoes over medium-high heat until tender, about 20 minutes.

Drain the potatoes in a colander, then return them to the pot and mash them with a potato masher or hand mixer. Add the milk, wasabi powder, butter, and wasabi peas and mash until well combined. Sprinkle with additional wasabi peas and serve hot.

Cranberry-Kaffir Lime Sauce

(Serves 6 or more)

4 cups fresh cranberries
1 cup sugar
2 teaspoons grated orange zest
*3 fresh kaffir lime leaves
    (available at Asian markets), finely shredded*

Combine all the ingredients with 1 cup water in a saucepan over low heat. Cook, stirring constantly, until the cranberries are soft and have just begun to split apart, about 15 minutes.

Remove from the heat and let the sauce cool for 5 minutes to allow it to gel. Serve warm.

Kabocha Pie

(Serves 6 or more)

*1 kabocha squash (2 to 3 pounds;
    available in most produce markets) or pumpkin*
*¾ cup palm sugar (also called jaggery;
    see Note; available at Asian markets),
    or 1 cup packed light brown sugar*
¼ cup coconut milk
4 large egg yolks
1 large egg
¼ teaspoon freshly grated nutmeg
*1 or 2 star anise, toasted in a dry pan
    for 2 to 3 minutes and ground in a spice mill*
1 baked 10-inch pie shell (page 92; make ½ recipe)
Vanilla Whipped Cream (page 149)

Preheat the oven to 300° F.

Peel and seed the squash and cut the flesh into 1-inch cubes. Cook it in boiling water for 10 minutes, then drain it and mash it in a mixing bowl. Let cool.

Combine the cooled squash with the palm sugar, coconut milk, egg yolks, whole egg, nutmeg, and ground star anise, stirring until smooth.

Pour the squash mixture into the pie shell and bake for 30 to 40 minutes; the filling should be set, but the middle should still tremble slightly when the pie is removed from oven. Refrigerate for at least 2 hours to chill completely. Slice the pie and serve each slice topped with a dollop of whipped cream.

NOTE: Palm sugar can be very hard. To loosen the sugar, microwave it for a few seconds in the jar, or in a heatproof bowl.

December in New York City

a hotel christmas and
a new year's eve black-and-white ball

Let me start by saying one thing: This country is full of amazing cities and towns, and there's no question that my entertaining philosophy has been influenced by each and every one of them. I'm talking about the whole nine yards, from the redwood forests to the Gulf Stream waters; or at least from Ioby's vineyard to Angelo and Lena's Miami spread. But, when I come home to New York for Christmas, I would be lying if I said my heart didn't skip a beat. A simple walk down Fifth Avenue becomes something as magnificently moving as the overture of a grand, spectacular Broadway musical—in color, in sound, in motion. Men in cashmere overcoats carry precarious towers of boxes as they hustle to the warmth of their homes; children with glowing faces huddle anxiously around the ornate holiday window displays of Macy's and Saks Fifth Avenue; women in matching hats and gloves alight out of the gold-trimmed doors of Bergdorf's, one hand clutching bundles of lavender bags and the other already raised for a taxi; steam rises up from the manhole covers, and the scent of roasting chestnuts swirls and billows around each street corner; the colored lights covering the tree at Rockefeller Center seem to illuminate the entire city with warmth and energy; snippets of Christmas carols emit in bursts through the whirl of revolving doors; and the windows of the bars and restaurants that line the sidewalk frame one scene of jovial cheer after another as patrons crowd together in warmth, comfort, and good spirits.

DID I MENTION THAT I love New York City at Christmastime? The exuberance and goodwill of the city make what should be, for an event planner, the most exhausting, hectic time of the year into a sheer joy. The holiday season becomes an energizing expression of my own excitement—which I never grew out of, even after I discovered that it was my parents who were gobbling up the cookies I left out by the chimney (nothing lasts forever, folks). And the whole thing reaches a stunning climax as the ball drops in Times Square, and people every-where huddle around their television sets to mark the coming of another great year in a great city. But we'll get to New Year's later. . . .

A Hotel Christmas
in the Big Apple

I take tree trimming very seriously. It's not just toss-ing a handful of tinsel on a pine tree; it's a ritual. Before I even bring the tree into my apartment, I make sure that Nat King Cole is on the stereo, cider is warming on the stove, and my favorite Christmas snack of Brie, figs, and date bread is beckoning from the counter. Only then do I undertake the position-ing of the tree, an almost curatorial endeavor that requires every little grain of feng shui know-how that I've picked up over the years.

I'm not sure that Carl and Emily knew exactly what they were getting into when they hired me to bring a little Christmas cheer into their temporary home at the Giraffe Hotel in Manhattan. But we turned out to be kindred spirits: Christmas enthusi-asts of the highest order. And so, as the contractors dismantled their Upper East Side home in the process of a renovation, we were building our own fantasy environment out of seemingly endless strands of colored lights, decorated sugar cookies, ribbons, hand-embroidered stockings, and home-made cider. Carl, whose love for Christmas puts even my own to shame (I didn't think it was possible), had called me with the concern that his two children, Sam and Suzanna, would be grinched out of a home-spun Christmas while staying in their temporary res-idence. I think my exact words to him were, "Why call it a temporary residence when you can call it a blank canvas ready to be filled with the details of a perfect Christmas?" I asked him how the family tra-ditionally celebrated Christmas, and, by the end of the conversation, we had decided to go ahead with the intimate, annual tree-trimming brunch that Carl thought he would have to forgo.

When the guests arrived for the holiday brunch and trimming of the tree, the essentials were in place. Boxes filled with tissue paper and ornaments waited beneath the tree like the early gifts they really are. The wafting aroma of coffee (Irish and regular) warmed the room, and the crackle of the fireplace served as a cozy soundtrack for this holiday occasion. As the children decorated the cookies with green and red sprinkles, and Emily placed her favorite teddy bears beneath the tree, I noticed the relieved expres-sion on Carl's face. I think both of us realized that it isn't really the decorations that make Christmas so special, but the moments of genuine connection between family and friends that they make possible. I have always stressed the importance of being a guest at your own party, not just a host, but holiday enter-taining almost requires the opposite: Let your guests do a little hosting themselves. For it is the collabora-tive nature of a good holiday party, where a guest might throw a log on the fire or pop another stick of cinnamon in the cider, that generates the essential spirit of generosity and togetherness.

Deck the Halls—the Walls, the Mantel, and the Hearth

My mother was always up in the attic weeks before Christmas carefully unpacking shiny gold ornaments and hand-embroidered stockings from folds of soft tissue. She considered every occasion an occasion for decorating the house, whether it was my brothers' *Star Wars*–themed birthday in the '70s or a Sunday Easter dinner for visiting relatives. But at Christmas, her skills with wrapping and caroling were something to stand back and admire. The ease with which she assembled centerpieces, wreaths, staircase garlands, mantelpiece displays of Christmas cards, red bows, and golden ornaments taught me one thing: Entertaining is always a pleasure, not a pressure.

For Carl and Emily's party it was not difficult to remember this motto. We hung custom stockings from the mantel, placed big jars of old-fashioned candy at child-height, filled glass hurricanes with gold and silver balls, made sugar cookies for eating and hanging on the tree, and topped the tree with exquisite ornaments. The room began to glow with a warm amber light, bathing us in holiday joy. Even a few of the decorating concepts I used here can transform an ordinary room into a Christmas wonderland. And remember, if you get started in early December, you can bathe in this glow for a full month.

The Holly and the Ivy

I am a sucker for a good Christmas tree. In fact, I often get two—as I did for Carl and Emily—one large tree for all the gifts and lights, and another smaller and complementary one for hanging cookies, cards, and homemade ornaments. But even if you just get one tree, you want it to last! These tough evergreens can dry out quickly and suddenly. Then, on Christmas Day, you've got bare, brittle branches and a pile of needles on the floor! Here are a few tree-preservation tips I learned from my mom and dad. They've been tested time and again and continue to work.

- Be sure to make a fresh, smooth cut to the trunk right before placing the tree into your stand. If you're buying a precut tree, ask the tree vendor to chop an extra inch off just before you bring the tree home.
- Add sugar to the water. It's true, even evergreens like a little sweetener!
- Water your tree! It gets thirsty, especially inside with the heater blasting.
- And speaking of heaters, do not position the tree too close to a radiator or heating vent. The heat will dry the pine needles right up.
- To prevent your tree from keeling over, make sure to evenly balance the lights and ornaments on all sides. This is especially true if the tree is in a corner and you are focusing on decorating one side.

Tree-Free: Alternative Holiday Foliage

Instead of (or in addition to) a big tree, alternative pine-colored plants can be added to create a cozy pine-scented holiday atmosphere in your home. Try small potted evergreen trees like holly, juniper, pine, cedar, boxwood, or laurel. If you live in a tropical climate and feel funny about forcing a wintry evergreen into your sun-kissed living room, try decorating with an abundance of red and white poinsettias and amaryllis. Both plants love the heat. As much as I love the idea in theory, in reality, holiday lights just don't work well with palms and banana trees. I'd avoid this particular look, original though it may sound.

Forest green and poinsettia red immediately connote the holidays, but sometimes all you need are a few striking winter-white bouquets to make a room shimmer like a winter wonderland. This is especially true if you're opting for white, instead of colorful, holiday lights. Some of my favorite white flowers are paper whites, white poinsettias, amaryllis, white roses, white hydrangeas, and white lilies.

Simple Holiday Chic

To bring your dining room into the holiday motif, pull out those summer hurricane lamps or cylindrical glass vases! Simply fill matching containers with different colored ornaments. I used gold, rust, and copper to match the tree design. This is a real fuss-free dining room design. These tubes of shimmering ornaments also look great on a hallway console table, clustered on a coffee table, on a fireplace mantel, or a buffet table. You can also leave this up after the holidays, through January.

Wrap It Up!

Sure, even presents wrapped in two-dollar drug-store wrapping paper look fabulous when piled up under the tree, but if you want to make a more personal and heartfelt statement, try these other ideas:

• Wrap presents with brown craft paper. Hand paint, stencil, or stamp decorations on the paper and finish with a festive bow.
• Cut out pages from holiday magazines and catalogs for wrapping smaller packages.
• To create extra-personalized wrapping paper, blow up old pictures from past Christmases and print them out on inexpensive paper. You can use a single enlargement or—if you're feeling ambitious—you can create a great photomontage or collage.
• Accent your gifts with ornaments, wrapped candies, ribbons, feathers, and even old-fashioned ribbon candy. You can also attach a card with your favorite Christmas cookie recipe.

• Wrap presents with white packing paper and let your children decorate them, creating a fun, personalized, and youthful look.

And remember, when cutting wrapping paper make sure to measure carefully, as excess paper creates a bulky look. After you make each cut, fold the paper under so you don't see any cut edges, creating a "tailored" look. Invest in a couple of rolls of double-sided, clear tape so your handiwork is literally invisible, and, if you love bows, try wire-edged ribbon, which is easier to manipulate and can curve and coil into beautiful shapes.

Trudy's Christmas Tree Cookies

(Makes about 2 dozen)

Suzanna and Sam helped me hang these cookies on the tree, though we nibbled a few in the process. Remember to make small holes before you bake so that you can thread a red ribbon through them for hanging.

2 sticks (1 cup) oleo or other margarine
  (oleo works best)
1½ cups confectioners' sugar
1 large egg
1 teaspoon vanilla extract
2½ cups all-purpose flour
1 teaspoon baking soda
1 teaspoon cream of tartar
¼ teaspoon salt
Icing and decorations of your choice

1. Cream the oleo in a large mixing bowl. Gradually add the confectioners' sugar and beat until the mixture is light and fluffy. Beat in the egg and vanilla until well combined.
2. In another bowl, combine the flour, baking soda, cream of tartar, and salt. Gradually add the dry ingredients to the wet ingredients, mixing until well combined. Form the dough into a ball, wrap in plastic wrap, and chill for at least 30 minutes.
3. Preheat the oven to 350° F.
4. Using a rolling pin, roll the dough out until it's ⅛ inch thick, then cut with your favorite cookie cutters. Using the tip of an ice pick or a plastic straw, pierce a hole near the top of each cookie (about ½ inch from the edge).
5. Bake on an ungreased cookie sheet for 5 to 8 minutes, until golden brown.
6. Let the cookies cool on a wire rack, then cover them with your favorite icing and decorations.

Molasses Christmas Crinkles

(Makes about 2 dozen)

Perfect for a party, these cookies, a Tutera family recipe, are as pretty as any ornament and taste like the perfect cookie combined with the perfect candy.

¾ cups vegetable shortening
1 cup packed light brown sugar
1 large egg
¼ cup molasses
2¼ cups sifted all-purpose flour
2 teaspoons baking soda
¼ teaspoon salt
½ teaspoon ground cloves
1 teaspoon ground cinnamon
1 teaspoon ground ginger
¼ cup granulated sugar, for dipping

1. In a large mixing bowl, thoroughly combine the shortening with the brown sugar, egg, and molasses.
2. In another bowl, combine the flour, baking soda, salt, cloves, cinnamon, and ginger. Add the dry ingredients to the wet ingredients, mixing until well combined. Cover the dough with plastic wrap and chill for at least 1 hour.
3. Preheat the oven to 375° F and grease a cookie sheet.
4. Roll the dough into balls the size of large walnuts. Dip the tops in the granulated sugar and place the balls, sugared side up and 3 inches apart, on the cookie sheet. Sprinkle each cookie with 2 or 3 drops of water to produce the cracked effect on the surface.
5. Bake the cookies for 10 to 12 minutes, or until they're just set, but not hard. Let the cookies cool on a wire rack.

Unique Traditions

Everyone has a favorite holiday tradition—for Emily and Carl, it is a traditional Christmas brunch. But every day—and every time of day—during the Christmas season offers a perfect excuse to spread holiday cheer. In addition to caroling parties, Christmas Eve dinners or that special Christmas brunch, you can:

• Host a merlot Christmas party: Ask your guests to bring a favorite bottle of merlot and invite them over for cookies, snacks, and tree trimming.

• Throw an all-dessert party, which can start later in the night, allowing guests to go to other parties first.

• Have a holiday cookie party where everyone brings a favorite batch of a cookie and its recipe.

• Host a gingerbread house party for kids. Bake sheets of gingerbread for the house as well as gingerbread men (and women!) and let the kids decorate.

Warming the Hearts of Your Guests...

These festive drinks will bring joy to any holiday party. In addition, serve mulled wine, a special treat specific to the holidays, and hot apple cider, also a wonderful substitution for your morning coffee or tea.

Warm "Big Apple" Pie

1 ounce spiced rum
1 ounce vanilla liqueur, preferably Xanath
5 ounces hot apple cider
Thin slice of red apple
Cinnamon stick

1. Pour the rum and vanilla liqueur into a coffee mug. Add the hot apple cider.
2. Garnish with the apple slice and cinnamon stick. Serve hot.

Crisp Kringle

1 ounce cranberry juice
Splash of white crème de menthe
3 ounces Moët & Chandon Champagne
Mint sprig

1. Pour cranberry juice, crème de menthe, and Champagne into a champagne glass.
2. Garnish with the sprig of fresh mint.

Mistletoe Martini

3 ounces Belvedere vodka
1 ounce cranberry juice
Splash of Chambord

TO SERVE
Lemon wedge
Red- and green-colored sugar
Fresh cranberries on a skewer

1. Rub a lemon wedge around the rim of a martini glass and dip one half into the red sugar and the other half into the green sugar.
2. Put the vodka, cranberry juice, and Chambord in a cocktail shaker with plenty of ice cubes.
3. Shake well and strain into the martini glass.
4. Garnish with the skewered cranberries.

Pepper Bloody Mary

1 ounce Belvedere vodka
6 ounces spicy Bloody Mary mix
½ teaspoon horseradish

TO SERVE
Lemon wedge
Coarse black pepper
Pickled green bean, green olive, and lime wedge on a skewer

1. Rub the rim of a Collins glass with a lemon wedge and dip it in the black pepper.
2. Add plenty of ice cubes and the vodka, Bloody Mary mix, and horseradish. Stir to combine.
3. Garnish with the skewered green bean, olive, and lime wedge.

Santa's Beard

This is a great treat for kids.

8 ounces cold cherry soda
2 scoops vanilla ice cream
Whipped cream
Peppermint stick

1. Pour the soda into a tall glass. Add the ice cream.
2. Top with whipped cream and garnish with the peppermint stick.

Three E's

Essentials
- Handmade Ornaments
- Holiday Cards Hanging on the Mantel or Tree
- Hot Cider, Mulled Wine

Extras
- Sugar Cookies for Decorating the Tree (and Eating!)
- Glass Cylinders Filled with Gold and Silver Ornaments
- Copper, Gold, and Rust-Colored Ornaments

Extravagances
- Hand-Embroidered Stockings
- Big Jars of Old-Fashioned Candy
- Antique Ornaments

TUTERA TIPS

• To create wonderful place mats to use at holiday dinner parties for years to come, glue old holiday cards into appropriately sized pieces of construction paper. Laminate these mats so that you can use them year after year.

• Purchase Christmas ornaments year-round whenever you travel. When Christmas season rolls around, you will be delighted to unwrap these treasures, which will add a wonderfully personalized—and worldly—touch to your tree.

• For a wonderful party favor for departing guests, fill a copper organza pouch with cinnamon sticks, cloves, and dried orange slices. Make sure to include recipes for how to turn these ingredients—and more—into holiday potpourri they can use at their own parties.

• As much as we all love receiving them, no one knows quite what to do with the stack of holiday cards we accumulate across this festive season. Here's one solution: Punch a hole in the top left corner of the cards, tie a pretty ribbon through them and hang them on the tree as an ornament. This is a tip from Mom if ever there was one!

• Send a Christmas ornament along with Christmas party invitations with the name of the guest and the word "joy" written in cursive on either side.

New Year's Eve Black-and-White Ball

After a year of designing party after party, you might think I'd celebrate the last night of the year by settling in for a night on the couch with Dick Clark and a carton of kung-pao chicken. Call me a glutton for punishment, or just a glutton for fun, but New Year's Eve is the only thing better than Christmas in my book, and I wasn't going to spend it carelessly. This annual extravaganza perfectly balances the nostalgia for a great year past with the hope of an even better year to come, and I am an unflinching optimist. And let's face it, New Year's Eve is THE party of the year. I love waking up on December 31st knowing that my only real responsibilities are to get dressed up, have a little too much Champagne and work it off as I dance into the new year. What a challenge!

In the lore of New York party history, one party stands out from the rest. Do I need to say it? Truman Capote's famous Black-and-White Ball. Although long gone are the days when you might find Andy Warhol, Norman Mailer, and Henry Kissinger milling around the same punch bowl, the spirit of such an encounter—and the party it makes possible—definitely lives on. Lucky for me, last New Year's Eve it lived on at the Black-and-White Ball I threw with my partner, Ryan. Norman Mailer wasn't provoking arguments with Italian ingenues, and Andy Warhol wasn't snapping Polaroids of Liza, but we all felt like superstars for a night.

Usually when I throw a party, the most formidable challenge is to find a way to transform the client's vision into reality. Iola's dream of a creative landscape became a room full of butterflies on the eve of the summer solstice; Caroline and Remy's love of Anne Rice novels became a lavish display of blood red roses and iron candelabras. For our own party, the challenge was to funnel all of our favorite impressions of New York City into one glamorous affair. And as Ryan and I mulled our favorite New York images—from the sleek grand piano at Bemelman's Bar to the Flatiron Building on a snowy morning to Audrey Hepburn's Givenchy dress and chunky pearls in *Breakfast at Tiffany's*—one theme emerged: Black and White. I mean, think about it: The striking lines of the Brooklyn Bridge lit up as if by fairy dust, the skyline at night illuminated by lights from within. This is a city of great dramatic contrasts. How could we bring it all into one room?

Having said that, a black-and-white color motif gets us only halfway there; the city has motion, too. We wanted our party to shimmy and shake like a Hot Box Girl from *Guys and Dolls* because formal parties, like formal gowns, need a little flourish. Ours came in the form of fluttering marabou feather boas. They lined the edges of lampshades, the hems of tablecloths, and the skirting of chair covers. And, naturally, the boas were white with black tips.

Of course, I have always believed that no party décor is complete until the guests have filled the room, and this was especially true for our party, which was brought to life by the black and white attire of the guests. As gentlemen mingled in their dashing tuxedos, the ladies slinked about in their sophisticated uptown ensembles. The feathers danced to the same rhythm as the guests, brought to life by the swish of a passing taffeta skirt. The whole affair was as simple and timeless as its inspiration: The first night of the future was beautiful.

An Extravagant End of Year Meal

I've obviously got a lot of favorite December-in-New-York associations, from Rockefeller Center to the image of Christmas presents spilling out of a bag in the backseat of a cab, but when it comes to eating New York dinner, I know where to go, Blue Hill Restaurant. Tucked away on the first floor of a nineteenth-century townhouse in the heart of Greenwich Village, this friendly, cozy (though thoroughly modern) restaurant always serves up an unforgettable meal. Over the years I've become acquainted with head chef, Dan Barber, and I've come to trust him to create outstanding menus for many of the events I produce. He loves what he does, and you can taste that passion in every bite of his food. He has a kind of youthful energy that seems to always be inspiring him to add that unusual twist to a recipe for fun, or drop a dollop of unexpected sauce to elevate a simple steak into culinary triumph.

I was thrilled that he agreed not only to prepare a menu for my black-and-white ball, but to show up in person and cook for us all! I knew that the year to come would be good, getting off to a start that included Fennel Soup with Shaved Black Truffle (it's New Year's Eve, let's splurge a little!); Poached Lobster with Shellfish Consommé, Braised Cabbage, and Turnips (turnips have never had it so good); and finally a perfect Rice Pudding with Sliced Grapes and Currants. This last, served in martini glasses, gave us a boost of energy to get out and dance the night (and year) away!

Invitation's in the Mail

Truman Capote had to hire an army of security guards to ensure that only authentic invitation-wielding A-listers made it into his black-and-white ball. Chances are, you will not need that kind of red-rope marshalling at your party, but you will want each of your guests to feel—from the moment they receive their invitation—that a party worthy of aggressive gate-crashing awaits them. Nothing says this better than a printed formal invitation. Remember, it's not just the degree of formality but also the style of the invitation that tells your guests exactly what to look forward to. In this case, fancy feather trim, chic Deco typeface, and playful wording informed our guests that they were in for a glamorous night infused with youthful energy. Each invitation was packaged in silver tissue and a small, lightweight box. Here we share some tips so you can make similarly spectacular invitations:

- Print the invitation text on white card stock.
- Glue two strips of white feathers to the back of the white card so that it appears, from the front, to be bordered on each side.
- Attach the feather-trimmed white card to a slightly larger black card.
- Slip the invitation into a silver, tissue-lined box that is only a tiny bit larger than the invitation. You don't want the invitation swimming around, hitting the edges of the box.
- Once in place, glue a few black feather tips to the interior lining of the box.
- In another larger box, mail, messenger-, or hand-deliver to your guests at least one full month in advance.

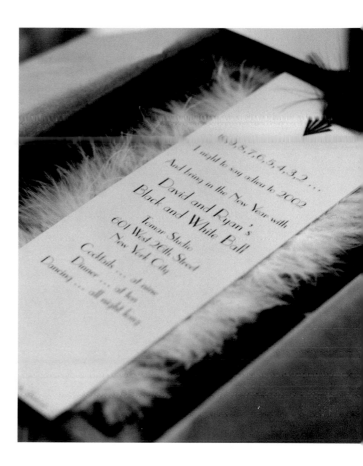

10, 9, 8, 7, 6, 5, 4, 3, 2 . . .

1 night to say adieu to 2002

And bring in the New Year with

David and Ryan's
Black and White Ball

Tomar Studio
601 West 26th Street
New York City

Cocktails . . . at nine
Dinner . . . at ten
Dancing . . . all night long

Kindly RSVP
This year . . . black tie glamour

A Black-and-White Location

Ryan and I wanted a completely blank slate on which to impose our black-and-white vision. What better place than a sparkling white, spacious photographer's loft? This was a perfect venue for us to create our party décor as Art. White floor, white walls, white ceiling, and a breathtaking view of the white lights would make the black-and-white carnations and feather boas stand out magnificently. If you want to host a Black-and-White Ball in your home, don't worry. You don't have to cover your abstract paintings and paisley cushions with white sheets. The truth is, even the most colorful environment will look wonderful once the black-and-white flowers, linens, feathers, striped café lamps, napkins, candles and—perhaps most importantly—the black-and-white glamour of your guests' formal attire fill the space!

New Year's Eve Journal

I often encourage my clients to provide guest books at momentous occasions such as New Year's Eve parties, weddings, engagement parties, and graduation parties. This year, Ryan and I decided to start a scrapbook of New Year's Eve parties. Ryan chose a lovely guest book and we encouraged our guests to write a personal wish, toast, or memory before leaving. After the party, we added a copy of the invitation, some photos, handwritten anecdotes, and even some funny drawings. Try this, and you'll be amazed: People genuinely like to join in and collaborate in any effort to preserve wonderful memories.

Marabou Feathers

Marabou feather boas add flair and whimsy to a formal party—just as they do to a formal gown. I prefer handmade marabou boas made with Turkish "fluff" feathers. They're easy to find (check the Internet!), ideal for cutting, gluing, or sewing, and they will not unravel easily. Marabou boas also look delightful when used for carnivals, Mardi Gras, Halloween, Christmas, or as an adornment to jackets, dresses, and lapels.

Café Lamps: Create "Holly Dolly" café lamps by pinning short lengths of marabou boas to the rim of a striped (or solid white) lampshade. Purchasing simple café lampshades means you will not have to worry about pinning tiny holes in one of your own precious shades. Simple café lampshades are affordable and easy to find at home design stores like Home Depot.

Hanging Lamp Shades: If you have hanging lights with large shades, you can easily wrap them with feather boas. To fasten them to a fixture, use small safety pins to hold the boas together and use strong, clear tape to attach each length of feathers to the shade. Do not adopt this method if the shade is close to the light bulb(s), or if the shade is glass and becomes very hot.

Tablecloth: Trim a black-and white-tablecloth with feathers. The look is like the edge of a dancer's skirt, mischievous and slinky. It's important to sew (or safety pin) the feathers tightly to the hem, so that gaps don't emerge. A gap in the trim not only looks bad, but it's a sure way to cause an accident. Avoid sewing pins too, as they might catch a dress hem or the stocking of a seated guest.

Chairs: Cover your rented chairs (for our party, we chose tall white stools) with sheer white covers and trim with . . . you guessed it, feathers! Ryan picked a sheer white fabric with tiny white polka dots and had the covers custom sewn. As the shapes of chairs vary, and the process can be somewhat complicated, I suggest asking a seamstress to do the trimming. The end result is stunningly elegant . . . with a touch of camp.

Centerpiece

The dining table was decorated with a magnificent runner of tall glass cylinders. Each displayed round spheres of black-and-white polka-dotted "pom-poms" made from carnations. Silver trays filled with shiny red apples not only accented this striking design but symbolized my hometown, the Big Apple. White tapered candles added height and elegance, as well as illuminated the carnations with a flickering of light. You can use most fluffy, strong, and straight-stemmed flowers to create pom-poms, but carnations are the most cost-effective for large displays.

- Purchase round Oasis balls (this green floral foam usually comes in rectangular bricks but is also available in round balls).
- Soak in water.
- Snip carnations with two inches of stem remaining.
- Insert carnations until the whole surface has been covered.

Pure Heaven

Ryan and I wanted the perfect white cocktail. And we didn't want milk involved! This year, we thought up this cocktail as our special drink to be offered as soon as guests arrive. Special cocktails add a personal touch, but remember to offer other drinks as well.

2 ounces vodka, preferably Belvedere
¾ ounce cream of coconut
¼ ounce pear nectar
Thinly sliced pear

1. Put the vodka, cream of coconut, pear nectar, and plenty of ice cubes in a cocktail shaker.
2. Shake well and strain into a chilled martini glass.
3. Garnish with a thin slice of pear.

Champagne Surprise

This is what I like to consider my signature cocktail. Not that I invented it, just that I serve it at every single party I host. It's pretty, bubbly, and has that smooth, clear kick you get from excellent vodka.

2 ounces vodka (I always use Belvedere)
1 ounce orange juice, stained to remove pulp and seeds
1 ounce Moët & Chandon Champagne
1 ripe blackberry

1. Pour the vodka and orange juice into a cocktail shaker filled with ice cubes.
2. Strain into a champagne flute and top with the Champagne.
3. Garnish with the blackberry.

It's All in the Timing!

I always suggest starting a New Year's Eve party a bit later, allowing the peak of your party to hit at midnight. This takes careful planning and timing. It's almost worth writing out a script for your party to help hone the timeline.

Here's a sample itinerary for New Year's Eve:

9:00—10:00	Cocktail hour
10:00—10:30	Cocktails continue in the dining area until...
10:30—11:00	Appetizer is served
11:00—11:30	Main course is served
11:30—12:00	Champagne poured; dancing begins
12:10—12:30	Coffee presented; dessert served
1:45 AM	Breakfast buffet opens for late-night phase of the partying (coffee, pastries, waffles, juices, and scrambled eggs)

I like things to flow and I like there to be things happening every 30 minutes so I keep my guests on their toes! Remember to nudge folks toward each new phase of the night enthusiastically and gently. In other words, avoid telling people what to do!

Three E's

Essentials
- White Votive Candles Lining the Entire Room and All Windowsills
- Silver Bowls of Red Apples
- White Carnations

Extras
- Rented Coatrack
- Black-and-White Printed Invitation with Feather Accent
- Black-and-White Striped Table Lamps

Extravagances
- Feather Boa–Trimmed Hanging Lampshades
- Carnation Pom-Poms
- Marabou Feather–Trimmed Tablecloth and Seat Covers

TUTERA TIPS

• Each place card can be a clock set at midnight with the guests' names attached. A wonderful place card and a perfect gift for guests to take home.

• Project black and white Hollywood silent films on the walls of your party to create a décor of beautifully photographed moving images.

• Introduce your guests to a wonderful Russian New Year's Eve tradition: Ask them to write a wish on a tiny piece of paper. At midnight each person swallows his or her wish, so that it will come true.

• For party favors, offer black-and-white cookies and apples covered in black-and-white chocolate as tasty reminders of a wonderful party!

• To add New York energy to your New York–style New Year's Eve party, serve a wonderful wine from a New York vineyard such as Banfi.

Reflecting on a Wonderful Year of American Parties: The Wrap Up

It wasn't until mid-January that I finally boxed up the tinsel, wrapped the ornaments in tissue, and hauled what may have been my best tree yet out to the chilly New York sidewalk. I felt a twang of nostalgia for the perfect month gone by as I stacked the last of the Christmas boxes in the storage closet, but I also felt a sense of comfort: The holidays are never over. Much like that tin of cheese and caramel flavored popcorn annually shipped from your aunt in Florida (which you not-so-secretly devour, practically in front of the postman), the Christmas season will keep on coming back around. In fact, it is this very quality, this eternal recurrence, that makes the holidays so special to us in the first place. Every year, I decorate a different tree with an ornament that my sister made for me in grade school, and every year I add a new ornament from someone dear to me. This year, Carl and Emily's children were kind enough to send me one of their creations. From now on, when I hang their sparkling star on my tree, I will be flooded with memories not only of their special holiday party, but of all the other amazing parties that made my year such a joy.

A lot of the people who hire me to throw parties think that their party is just like any other as far as I'm concerned. Nothing could be farther from the truth. I've already expressed the comfort I take in the knowledge that the holidays return year after year, and that each time they do, they bring new people into my life, and new memories to go with them. I throw parties for the same reasons. No matter how many Valentine's Day celebrations I plan, each of them remains fresh for me. I learn something new from every client I work with, and every time I use an old trick it finds new life. As I travel from city to city, I not only tap into the essence of the location, but the spirit of the people. I have the honor of finding concrete expression for the dreams of others, and that is no small honor; my learning experience is perpetual and cyclical, and it deepens with every returning occasion.

On New Year's day, I had an amazing night to reflect on. Toby had surprised us with two cases of his finest vintage wines. Watching the first snow of the year fall over the city's skyline while sharing these exquisite bottles with Ryan and our guests had a major effect on us. For them, it brought the best of America's two coasts together in one great moment; for me, it brought my whole year together. All the miles I'd traveled between Ojai and Greenwich Village, New Orleans and Nantucket, and all the parties I'd helped bring to life along the way, came flooding back to me. I realized that at that moment I was actually listening to one of the jazz compilations I had mixed for Ted's Chicago cocktail party; I was recognizing the inner topiary (pure Washington, D.C.) of my carnation centerpiece; and I was trying desperately to channel Lena's grace as I moved toward the dance floor. Parties are for me the deepest kind of connection with people, places, and dreams. As the clock struck midnight, confetti filled the air, and corks popped, I wished only for another year so full of passion for all of life's little celebrations.

December in New York City
MENU

Courtesy of Dan Barber,
chef at Blue Hill Restaurant.

Fennel Soup *with Shaved Black Truffle*

Poached Lobster *with Shellfish Consommé and Braised Cabbage and Turnips*

Rice Pudding *with Sliced Grapes and Currants*

Fennel Soup *with Shaved Black Truffle*
(Serves 6)

$2\frac{1}{2}$ teaspoons vegetable oil
$\frac{1}{2}$ small Spanish onion, chopped
2 shallots, peeled and chopped
$2\frac{1}{2}$ teaspoons fennel seeds
$1\frac{1}{2}$ bulbs fennel, chopped, tops discarded
$1\frac{1}{2}$ cloves garlic, chopped
$4\frac{1}{2}$ cups rich chicken stock, preferably homemade
Salt and freshly ground pepper to taste
1 ounce black truffle

Heat the oil in a saucepan over medium heat. Add the onion and shallots and gently cook until translucent and glossy, being careful not to brown them, 2 to 3 minutes. Add the fennel seeds and cook for 1 minute. Add the fennel and cook for 4 to 5 minutes. Stir in 3 cups of the stock and simmer until the fennel is very tender, about 15 minutes.

Heat the remaining $1\frac{1}{2}$ cups stock in a second saucepan.

Carefully pour the fennel soup into a blender—it'll be very hot—and puree; you may need to do this in batches.

Strain the soup through a fine-mesh sieve or chinois and return the pureed soup to the saucepan. If necessary, thin the soup with the remaining stock. Season with salt and pepper to taste.

Pour the soup into warmed individual serving bowls. Generously shave the black truffle on top and serve hot.

Poached Lobster *with Shellfish Consommé and Braised Cabbage and Turnips*
(Serves 6)

6 lobsters (6 to 8 pounds total)
1 onion, diced
1 carrot, peeled and diced
1 bulb fennel, diced, tops discarded
1 rib celery, diced
2 cloves garlic, minced
1½ cups white wine
3 sprigs fresh thyme
3 sprigs fresh tarragon
3 quarts fresh carrot juice
1 recipe Beurre Blanc (recipe follows)
2 cups diced turnips, blanched for 1 minute
  in heavily salted boiling water
1 head savoy cabbage, leaves separated,
  blanched for 1 minute in salted boiling water,
  and cut into thin strips
Salt and freshly ground pepper to taste

Remove the tails and claws from the lobsters and set aside. Clean the lobster heads and chop the lobster bodies into 4 pieces. Bring a large pot of water to a boil and fill a large bowl with ice water. Being careful not to overcook, blanch the lobster tails in the boiling water for 3 minutes and the claws for 5 minutes. Immediately transfer them to the ice-water bath to cool. Remove the lobster meat from the tails and claws and set aside.

In a large pot over medium heat, gently cook the onion, carrot, fennel, celery, and garlic until the onion is translucent, 3 to 5 minutes. Add the lobster bodies, increase the heat to medium-high, and cook until they turn red, 5 to 7 minutes. Add the wine and simmer until the liquid is reduced by three-quarters. Stir in the herbs and carrot juice and simmer for about 30 minutes. Remove and discard the lobster bodies, then strain the consommé through a fine-mesh sieve and set the consommé aside.

Cut the lobster tail meat pieces in half. Add the tail meat and claw meat to the saucepan with the Beurre Blanc and heat them gently over medium-low heat, about 5 minutes, being careful not to bring the Beurre Blanc to a boil.

When it's time to serve, heat the turnips and cabbage in about ½ cup of the consommé and season with salt and pepper to taste. Reheat the rest of the consommé in another saucepan. Divide the cabbage and turnips among warmed serving bowls—pasta bowls work well. Place the meat of 1 lobster tail and 2 claws in each bowl. Serve immediately, ladling the hot consommé over the poached lobster at the table.

Beurre Blanc
(Makes about 3 cups)

2 cups white wine
2 sprigs fresh thyme
2 shallots, peeled and thinly sliced
[illegible] heavy cream
2 pounds (8 sticks) cold unsalted butter, cut into cubes
Salt and freshly ground white pepper to taste

In a medium saucepan over medium-high heat, combine the wine, thyme, and shallots; bring to a simmer and cook until the mixture is almost dry, about 12 minutes. Add the cream and cook until the mixture is reduced to 2 cups. Strain through a fine-mesh sieve or chinois and return the sauce to the pan.

Lower the heat to medium-low. Using a hand mixer or whisk, add the cold butter, incorporating it piece by piece. Do not let the sauce boil. Season with salt and pepper and serve warm.

Rice Pudding
with Sliced Grapes and Currants
(Serves 6)

1½ pounds Arborio rice
2 vanilla beans split in half lengthwise
2 cinnamon sticks
3 cups heavy cream
3 cups whole milk, plus more if necessary
2¼ cups sugar
2¼ cups mascarpone cheese

TO SERVE
Sliced seedless purple grapes
Fresh currants, on the stems (optional)

Bring 1½ quarts water to a boil in a large saucepan. Add the rice and blanch it for 3 minutes. Drain the rice in a fine-mesh sieve, rinse it briefly with cold water to remove excess starch, and return it to the saucepan.

Add the vanilla beans, scraping the seeds into the pan, the cinnamon, cream, milk, and sugar, stirring to combine. Bring the mixture to a boil, then reduce the heat to low. Gently simmer, stirring every 3 to 4 minutes, for about 30 minutes, or until the rice is tender.

Remove the pudding from the heat and stir in the mascarpone cheese, thinning the pudding with a little more milk, if needed.

Spoon the warm rice pudding into 6 individual serving bowls and garnish with the sliced grapes and a bunch of currants.

The Restaurants

January in Miami

Larios on the Beach
Pedro Maradiago, chef
820 Ocean Drive
Miami Beach, FL 33139
305-532-9577

February in New Orleans

Emeril's Restaurant
Christopher Wilson, chef
800 Tchoupitoulas Street
New Orleans, LA 70130
504-528-9393

March in Aspen

Hotel Jerome
Todd Slossberg, chef
Summer—The Garden Terrace
Winter—The Century Room
330 East Main Street
Aspen, CO 81611
970-920-1000

April in Southern California

Mélisse
Josiah Citrin, chef and owner
1104 Wilshire Boulevard
Santa Monica, CA 90401
310-395-0881

May in Kansas City

40 Sardines
Michael Smith, head chef and co-owner, and
Debbie Gold, pastry chef and co-owner
11942 Roe Avenue
Overland Park, KS 66209
913-451-1040

June in Santa Fe

The Compound
Mark Kiffin, chef and owner
653 Canyon Road
Santa Fe, NM 87501
505-982-4353

July in Washington, D.C.

Melrose at the Park Hyatt Hotel
Brian McBride, chef
1201 Twenty-fourth Street, NW
Washington, D.C. 20037
202-789-1234

August in Nantucket

Brant Point Grill at the White Elephant
Donald Kolp, executive chef
50 Easton Street
Nantucket, MA 02554
508-228-2500

September in Charleston

The Peninsula Grill at Planters Inn
Robert Carter, chef
112 North Market Street
Charleston, SC 29401
843-723-0700

October in Dallas

The French Room at the Adolphus
William Koval, executive chef
1321 Commerce Street
Dallas, TX 75202
214-742-8200

November in Chicago

Arun's
Arun Sampanthavivat, chef and owner
4156 North Kedzie Avenue
Chicago, IL 60618
773-539-1909

December in New York City

Blue Hill Restaurant
Dan Barber, chef
75 Washington Place
New York, NY 10011
212-539-1776

Recipe Index

"The party's over..."

Mary Corsaro